SAVING SACRAMENTO

Published by Price World Publishing
1300 W Belmont Ave Ste 20G
Chicago, IL 60657-3200
www.PriceWorldPublishing.com

Cover Photo by Patrick Lucas
Cover Design by Russell Marleau
Layout Design by Merwin Loquias
Interior Photos by Patrick Lucas
Editing by Vanessa Fravel
Printing by United Graphics

ISBN: 9781932549836
eBook ISBN: 9781619843455
Library of Congress Control Number: 2013912908

Printed in the United States of America
10 9 8 7 6 5 4 3 2 1

For information about discounts for bulk purchases,
please contact info@priceworldpublishing.com.

SAVING SACRAMENTO

KEEPING THE KINGS IN THE CAPITAL

A STORY OF

FANS, SPORTS & POLITICS

JASON COLDIRON

PRICE WORLD
PUBLISHING

CONTENTS

PREFACE

y name is Jason Coldiron. I am a sportswriter with a passion for the Kings. For two years I was the number one Sacramento Kings writer on Bleacherreport.com. For more than 30 years I have lived in Sacramento and its surrounding areas and have followed the Sacramento Kings since their arrival in 1985. I have met coaches and players of the team, been to rallies and press conferences, and seen up-close what a sports franchise can do for a city. I even watched or listened to every single Kings game from 1991 to 2006 and most of them since. In this book I've included a handful of appendices to provide additional insight and information about certain topics. For additional information about me and my love of the Kings, see Appendix 1.

The team has been a source of passion, love, pain and, more recently, frustration for me. My memories of going to Kings games with my father as a child are some of the best memories of my life. For years, my father and I had season tickets to watch one of the worst teams in the league. I lived through years of the team being terrible in the 80's and 90's. I watched them as they were often the laughingstock of the NBA, including going 1-40 in road games for an entire season (1990-91). I endured the ridicule of other kids in school when they were an embarrassment. The team suffered for years under bad ownership and bad play on the court. Eventually the team was sold to the Maloof family.

The next decade brought what would come to be called: "The Greatest Show on Court" by *Sports Illustrated*. The team went on to great success for a period of several years and appeared to be thriving. With all the success they were having, it was easy for most of the country and the sports world to miss what was happening behind the scenes. The events that were happening in press conferences and town hall meetings, deciding the fate of the city, led to the events of 2013, specifically. The end result is that the Sacramento Kings franchise has been sold to a new ownership group which, in conjunction with the city of Sacramento, will build a new sports and entertainment complex in downtown Sacramento. This is the end-game outcome the city has been looking for more than 15 years.

I know what an amazing opportunity this is for the city of Sacramento, the NBA and the local economy in general. For years I tried to spread the message of the importance of the situation to friends, coworkers, strangers and anyone who would listen. As I explained the story and the situation to people, over and over, something bothered me: many of the people in this city did not seem to understand how big a deal this was. They didn't understand how an NBA team in a city affects all of its residents' lives. I felt like I was shouting from a mountain trying to make people understand. I failed so many times in trying to effect change in the minds of people I met. Even many of my friends and family in the area didn't understand. Many times I spoke to groups of friends for hours, thinking I was helping, only to find at the end that most of the people I spoke to still didn't get it. I nearly gave up trying to spread the message, but I never gave up hope.

"Who cares about basketball?"

"The Kings suck anyway, let them go."

"Sports owners and players are greedy bastards. Why should the city help build them an arena so they can just keep getting richer?"

These are the kinds of comments I heard over and over and over again. I wanted to scream at people. I wanted to make them understand that this is about so much more than basketball. That it not only affects every resident of this community, but its reach includes all of California and the sports world.

When our country has an election and names a president every four years, many people vote for the other guy, the one that loses. When the president does good things, everyone benefits, even those who did not vote for him. In the same way, the people in this town that have been opposed to a new arena will also get to enjoy the benefits of it for at least the next 35 years. They will reap the benefits of an improving economy, a thriving area downtown, more businesses, more investments, more jobs, more opportunities and a better way of life in Sacramento.

Over the course of the last decade or so, team owners and city leaders failed to educate the public properly. I believe this was the biggest obstacle and biggest reason it took so long to do something (build an arena) that is so clearly good for the city and its residents.

In time, people will understand what happened here and why their lives are better. That understanding is the purpose of this book.

INTRODUCTION

*I*n May of 2013, NBA owners rejected a bid to move the Sacramento Kings franchise to Seattle. Prominent investor Chris Hansen had made an agreement to buy the team from the Maloof family and move them to the Pacific Northwest. Hansen fought to the bitter end to acquire the team. He even negotiated to buy a minority share when it became clear the league opposed relocation.

With relocation rejected by the league, the Maloofs were forced to either keep the Kings franchise in Sacramento while continuing to own the team themselves (not a pleasant thought for any of the parties involved), or to sell to a group of investors put together by Mayor Kevin Johnson that would keep the team in town. That decision came quickly: just one day after NBA owners officially rejected the bid to relocate the Kings to Seattle, the Maloofs agreed to sell the Kings to investors who would keep the team in Sacramento.

Software billionaire Vivek Ranadive and his group of investors came to an agreement to purchase 65 percent of the Kings from the Maloof family for approximately $348 million. The Kings' total valuation in the sale was $535 million, an NBA record (even though the Kings were one of the least-coveted franchises in the league).

Kevin Johnson announced to screaming throngs of Kings fans on Friday, May 17th 2013 that the deal to sell the NBA franchise to Ranadive's group had been signed. The future plan for the

Kings now includes a $447 million downtown arena that will be built at the western gateway to the city near the Sacramento River.

The announcement at a City Hall rally brought an end to years of maneuvering by Johnson to secure a new ownership group, convince the Sacramento city council to commit to building a new downtown arena, and show the NBA that the capital city of the most populous state in the nation has the fan base to make the venture successful.

This is the Sacramento that I know and love, just off the freeway on J Street. The right side of this street is going to look very different in the coming years.

More importantly, the announcement brought relief to a community that had been caught in the middle of the situation for years. It became an historic day for this city and an awful lot of people.

As a sports fan, the saving of the Kings thrilled me, but this is much bigger. New ownership and a new arena downtown is the culmination of years of effort and agony by a large group of individuals. It is also a major victory for a city that desperately needed one. It is truly an amazing series of events with a happy ending for Sacramento and for the NBA. In light of all this, 2016 looks really bright for the Kings and the league.

While there is glory to be had in Sacramento, it is also important to understand that there are both winners and losers in this series of events.

The NBA comes out ahead because one of the least coveted franchises in their league sold for more money than their most expensive franchise was previously worth. More importantly, the NBA wins because they get to look like the good guys. Allowing the Kings to relocate to Seattle would have represented the opposite image they tried to portray for themselves during the 2011 lockout that cost nearly half of the 2011-12 NBA season. During that time, the owners had represented themselves as the victims, needing reform to make their business profitable for all its franchises.

Just two years removed and it is already clear that the owners got the better of the players in the 2011 negotiations. The players lost so badly that they are suing their own union leadership. They gave up just over 6% of all BRI (Basketball-related Income), along with more contract rules favorable to teams and not players. Players now only get maximum length contracts of four and five years (depending on length of service), two less than in the previous collective bargaining agreement (CBA). In the previous CBA, players could get six-year contracts with 10.5 percent raises for Bird free agents; five years with 8 percent raises for other players. In the new CBA, players can only get five-year contracts with 7.5 percent raises for Bird free agents; four years with 4.5 percent raises for other players. To top it all off, players lost about 20 percent of their 2011-12 salaries as a result of the games missed due to the lockout.

Meanwhile, team values are skyrocketing. Some for business reasons, some for prestigious reasons. The average NBA team is now worth around $370 million. In 2011, Forbes had the Sacramento Kings franchise' valued at $293 million. In 2013 they were sold for $535 million. In 2011, Ted Leonsis purchased the other 56% of the Washington Wizards and Verizon Center that he did not already own, plus the Baltimore-Washington D.C. Ticketmaster franchise. The sale put a valuation on the team of $551 million (and that was for the Wizards!). It may have been true at the time that the owners as a whole had a couple of seasons in the red, but that was just the recession talking. The owner's cries of poverty were widely overblown and their teams are all worth fortunes. Still, they got the players to bend over to their every wish. The owners' win may go down as one of the greatest corporate victories in labor-law history.

Taking a team away from a loyal fan base in a small market would have made the NBA look like the bad guys and, as they determined on their own, would have been bad for business. It also helps their business model to have another city use taxpayer money to build an arena from which they will largely benefit. *There is another line of thought that suggests owners want all their arenas to be financed by their cities. Some even suggest that Chris Hanson's willingness to pay for most of the Seattle team with private funds was actually a negative in the eyes of the other owners.*

Seattle becomes a loser in the short-term, but a winner in the big picture. True, they did not get an NBA team at this time, but their efforts have essentially guaranteed they will eventually get one. There is much to be said for Seattle losing the SuperSonics in 2006 and this book will address that. It is true that they had their team taken from them unfairly, but creating a second wrong would not help anything. There is still hope for Seattle, as there are other teams in similar situations as Sacramento coming up in the next few years. Situations in Milwaukee and Minnesota, for instance, have that kind of potential. While a move from any other city could be a second wrong, the league will still have Seattle and Hansen as a leverage city to get what they want elsewhere. The league has said for years that expansion will never be an option again. Many experts claim that for the NBA to continue to succeed it actually needs to contract a couple of teams, not expand. That said, the efforts of Seattle and Hanson have ensured that they will eventually get another team. Money talks and Hanson has enough to win a conversation eventually.

Sacramento wins for several reasons.

For one, sports fans win. Sacramento is a one-team pro sports town. The Kings get 100 percent of the local sports and entertainment draw. The thousands of fans who grew up in this town win; we get to keep our memories. We get the chance to pass the love of the game on to the next generation. **The game is special and Sacramento is a place where it is loved.** It should be here. Now it will be forever.

The city also gains by ridding themselves of having to deal with the Maloof family ever again.

The Sacramento economy wins most of all. As of this moment, revitalization of downtown Sacramento looks like a reality in fall of 2016. New ownership brings a new arena deal, jobs, entertainment, and all the restaurants, stores, bars and other businesses that benefit from the presence of the Kings. It also helps Sacramento in terms of civic pride and prestige.

Most of all, the people of Sacramento win. All the grassroots efforts that the city stepped up with over the last few years paid off, led by the now-legendary Carmichael Dave. The people of this town went through so much for so long and our suffering has finally paid off. I didn't have to explain to my son why the team is leaving and how ultimately money talks loudest. In a world where it seems the big guys always win, this time the people won.

The series of events that led to this moment are numerous, far-reaching and worth extensive examination. This book seeks to understand, evaluate and explain the amazing series of events and people that made it happen. This is a story about sports and economics but, above all, it is a story about people.

THE KEY PARTIES

KEVIN JOHNSON

*K*evin Maurice Johnson is the current mayor of Sacramento, which is the capital city of the state of California. Johnson was elected in 2008 and re-elected in 2012, primarily because he would do everything in his power to get a new arena built in Sacramento and keep the Kings forever.

This is the reason why I think he was elected, anyway. I am told that there are other, bigger, reasons he was elected.

Kevin Johnson was born on March 4, 1966 in Sacramento. He was raised here and went to Sacramento High School. He played basketball in college and then had a storied career in the NBA. With the Phoenix Suns, he was one of the most feared offensive players of his era. He is a story of local success. He is a hometown hero who came back to save the city. In his time in office he has clearly demonstrated a love for the community and a commitment to improving it through his efforts and causes. He is one of the great success stories in the history of this city and it is fitting that he is now mayor.

Some of Johnson's efforts include: *Volunteer Sacramento* (2009), *For Art's Sake* (2010), *Sacramento Steps Forward* (2009), *Stand Up* (2009), *Greenwise* (2010), *Sacramento Reads* (2011), *City-Schools Collaborative* (2011), and *Gang Prevention Task Force* (2011).

While the function of many of these programs is obvious from their names, they, along with other efforts, serve to support and improve Sacramento in a number of ways. The programs address homelessness (which is among the worst in the country), improve education and bring education reform, improve the economy and raise awareness for all of these issues.

In my humble opinion, the most important of the groups he created was *Think Big* (2010). Johnson launched this project to: "Facilitate the economic development of Sacramento, including the construction of a new entertainment and sports complex." The goal of this group could also be stated another way: "To keep the Kings in Sacramento." While some people might believe that gang prevention, education and homelessness are more important than a sports arena, I believe that is a shortsighted view. Just as it may be true that high school music and math clubs may be arguably more important than football in themselves, it is also true that sometimes clubs like these would not exist without the football team. In the same way, education and homelessness are huge problems for the city, but the arena and basketball team will affect the whole area in ways that will improve those problems in a bigger way, creating more resources that can be used to improve even more situations.

Mayor Johnson's efforts since his election are the reason Sacramento still has the Kings.

On a personal note, I met Kevin Johnson when I was ten years old. He was doing an autograph signing at a local high school. My dad took me there to meet him and I brought my Topps basketball card

*for him to sign. I was too shy to speak to him, but he said 'thanks'
as he signed my card.*

THE MALOOF FAMILY

*T*he Maloof family is originally from New Mexico, although for all intents and purposes they are a Las Vegas family. The family's success began with the distributing rights of Coors Beer in the Southwest region of the US in 1937. It was from this highly successful distribution service that the family was able to build their empire. The Maloofs were the owners of the Sacramento Kings from 1998 until 2013. The family consists of George J. Maloof, his wife Colleen, and their children: Adrienne Maloof-Nassif, Joe Maloof, Gavin Maloof, George J. Maloof Jr and Phil Maloof.

The family acquired a minority interest in the Kings in 1998 and took majority control the following year, with Joe and Gavin operating the franchise. As part of the purchase of the Kings, they also acquired the team's sister franchise in the WNBA, the Sacramento Monarchs. The Maloofs operated the Monarchs until 2009, when the WNBA was unable to find a new owner and the team folded. (*Ironically, the Monarchs won a title and the Kings still never have*)

The Maloofs had a family history with the NBA before the Kings. They briefly owned the Houston Rockets from 1979-1982. They sold the team to Charlie Thomas in 1982. Around the time they bought the Kings, they said that they had always regretted selling the Rockets and that buying back into the NBA was their life's dream. There was much melodrama and it seemed to be a match made in heaven.

For the Maloof brothers, owning an NBA team was a special thing for a time. For years, they would sit courtside at almost every game, decked out in Kings jerseys, walking around the lower deck and connecting with their fans the way few owners do. As the team went through a steady decline on the court over the last six years, the love affair ended and the Maloofs became infrequent visitors to ARCO Arena (renamed a few times since and currently called Sleep Train Arena), the Kings' home since 1988. And when they did show up, they sat in a luxury box, segregated from the fans.

In 1994, four years before buying the Kings, the Maloof family had expanded their empire when they bought the Fiesta Hotel in Las Vegas for $8 million. They sold it in 2000 for over $185 million. They reinvested the money into the creation of The Palms hotel and casino in Vegas. This seemed like a successful venture at the time, but it turns out the Maloofs' run of good fortune and good business was heading to an end.

With the economy in a major recession and all of their businesses doing poorly, the Maloofs eventually sold their beer distribution in an unsuccessful attempt to save the Palms and Palms Towers. Their slide didn't stop. They then sold the majority of their stake in the Palms to TPG Capital and Leonard Green & Associates. The Maloofs were left with two percent ownership. The Palms is now going through a re-branding led by Joe Magliarditi.

The Maloofs have since expanded their business ventures into entertainment with the creation of Maloof Productions and Maloof Music, with the hope of developing and producing film and television projects. So far, Maloof Productions has produced the reality series *Bullrun* for Spike TV in 2007, Speed Channel in 2009, and *Living Lohan* for E!, which ran in 2008. They are currently developing *Rebuilding the Kingdom* with reality television producer Mark Burnett. *I suspect that project may have gone out the window with their sale of the Kings, but we shall see.*

The Maloofs have owned the Kings in Sacramento since 1999. They've cheered with Sacramento, wept with Sacramento, sweated with Sacramento, cursed the skies (and refs) with Sacramento. Despite this, there is one key reality that needs to be understood: the Maloofs never really loved Sacramento, despite all their claims over the years to the contrary. Maybe in the beginning they liked it here. Maybe they gave it a chance. Maybe if the city had ponied up money for the extravagant arena they wanted, they would have lived here happily ever after. None of those things happened. Instead, they tried to leave a few times, officially beginning in 2006. In 2011 they thought they had found an exit strategy: they would move the team to Anaheim. The deal seemed to be done until Sacramento stepped up to stop them.

The Maloofs never forgave Kevin Johnson and Sacramento for making them stay here. From 2006 forward, they wished for no peace with Sacramento, instead looking to make money, even at the expense of the city and fan base that helped them become so rich and supported them for years. They stopped investing in the team on the court and the team became terrible. During the 2012-13 season they even traded away their first round draft choice, Thomas Robinson, for basically $3.5 million in savings for them.

In some ways, I still don't truly understand many of their decisions and behavior. (Appendix 2)

This comes after years of inept businesses behavior by the Maloofs. There was the insulting Carl's Jr. commercial in 2006 that the Maloofs didn't seem to realize was a big deal. There was the time they torpedoed a proposed tax in Sacramento that would have helped them get the arena they wanted. There were four years when they were making personal calls to season-ticket holders to ask them to renew their tickets at the same time they were negotiating deals to move the team to Anaheim and Seattle. There was the backing out of the Sacramento deal in 2012. There was the denying for years that the team was for sale while they were clearly shopping the team around. There is the fact that they never offered to sell to local ownership until it became their last option. Then, as the events of 2013 played out, there was George Maloof hiding in a hotel closet and then standing on his hotel balcony yelling down to reporters about how great Chris Hanson is.

The Kings, under the Maloof's guidance, are one of two NBA teams (along with the Minnesota Timberwolves) not to make the playoffs since the 2005-06 season. (Appendix 3) According to the ESPN 2012 Ultimate Team Rankings, in just nine years, the Sacramento Kings have dropped from number 4 to number 121 out of 122 sports franchises, based on a number of categories including ownership (ranking dead last), stadium experience and fan relations. This underlines the fact that the Maloofs gave up on Sacramento.

Given the way the Maloofs had torched the image of the league by slashing payroll, putting a poor product on the floor, and fighting against the wishes of the NBA for the past few years, they stood little chance of ever getting what they wanted. Hanson and Seattle would be their last hope to find a golden parachute. If that didn't work, they would have to choose between making the best of their situation here, or spending another decade spitting on Sacramento and its fans.

Mayor Johnson has said all the right things about the Maloofs. He has been quick to remind people about all the good things the Maloof brothers have done for the Sacramento area, including giving almost $20 million to organizations and groups in the area. Once the deal to keep the Kings in Sacramento was eventually done, Johnson was still gracious, saying, "They didn't have to accept the backup offer, and they did."

After the sale was final, Gavin Maloof said, "Perhaps one day we'll have another opportunity, maybe in another sport, to get back into it. You never know. Right now, we'll take a deep breath and a step back." [1]

That statement belies the ignorance of the Maloof family. After what they have done in Sacramento they will never be allowed to own a sports franchise ever again. The Maloof family was once rich and powerful. As of May 2013 they are the laughingstock of the sports world and severely diminished in the business world.

Personally, I defended these people for years. I saw their position as businessmen and defended them and their right to make money. I can face the truth now: they are simply not very good businessmen. By now, the Maloofs must know they are not well liked in Sacramento, but I doubt they realize how much. I do not hate them by any stretch, but there are some in this town who will for a very long time.

THE FANS (AND THEIR RESPONSIBILITY)

One aspect of the situation that is often overlooked is the fans' responsibility in what happens to teams they love. Whether they stay or go is ultimately because of fans. League executives, millionaire investors and government officials sign the deals that make things happen. Their decisions are based on how they can make the most money possible. In the case of owning an entertainment business such as a basketball team, they want to know how committed the fans are to continuing to give them their money for a long time. The situations in Seattle and Sacramento present two different examples of how fan behavior can affect business behavior.

In the events of 2013, Seattle was the city trying to get a team, but that was not the case just a few years ago. Seattle had a well-respected team and organization in their SuperSonics. They were a team with a solid history in the city and the league. Sam Schulman was the original owner of the team from its birth in 1967 until 1983. They were next owned by Barry Ackerley from 1983-2001. Then came the ownership group headed by Starbucks chairman Howard Schultz and his 58 partners and minority owners.

Schultz was considered by many to be a man running a business, not a team or organization. While some criticized his commitment to fielding a winning team, the organization as a whole enjoyed profitability and moderate success on the court under Schultz's leadership. Schultz tried for years to convince the city of Seattle to provide public funding to build a new arena to replace the aging Key Arena. He watched the city use public money to build new facilities for both the Seahawks and Mariners over the years. He saw the prosperity it brought both of those teams and wondered why the city would not help him. Perhaps he overlooked the fact that Seattle had already paid an astounding 200 million dollars during the 90s to renovate the Key Arena? Perhaps the fact that the city is still paying for those renovations today matters? Seattle was being asked to build a new arena when they hadn't even come close to paying for renovations on the one they already had. The city was not ready to invest even more money in the NBA.

Eventually, Shultz reached his breaking point and decided to move on to other ventures. He sold the SuperSonics to Clayton Bennet and his ownership group based in Oklahoma City for $350 million on July 18, 2006. Schultz said he sold the franchise to Bennet's group because he thought that Bennet would not move the franchise to Oklahoma City. The sale to the out-of-state owners destroyed Schultz's popularity in Seattle. In one local newspaper poll, Schultz was judged most responsible for the team leaving the city.

It is very important to consider the ramifications of Shultz's actions. The problem wasn't that he had sold the team. The problem was that he had sold it to someone who clearly would leave town as soon as possible or faster if he could. The sale of the team to Clay Bennet really meant that Seattle would lose their beloved SuperSonics.

To understand the pain of Seattle fans it is important to fully understand how badly they were lied to. At the time of the team's sale, Bennet and the new owners claimed they would work with the city of Seattle to build a new arena and only consider moving the team as a last resort. Emails were later obtained by the city showing communications between NBA commissioner David Stern and Bennett on Aug. 17, 2007, in which Bennett insisted he'd never spoken to his partners about moving the team out of Seattle. That claim contradicted an April 17 email exchange between Bennett and Sonics co-owners Aubrey McClendon and Tom Ward. In that exchange, the three gleefully talked about getting the team to Oklahoma City as quickly as possible. The conversation is shocking.

Bennet wrote David Stern in August of 2007, "You are just one of my favorite people on earth and I so cherish our relationship, Sonics business aside. I would never breach your trust. As absolutely remarkable as it may seem, Aubrey (McClendon) and I have NEVER discussed moving the Sonics to Oklahoma City, nor have I discussed it with ANY other member of our ownership group. I have been passionately committed to our process in Seattle, and have worked my ass off. The deal for me has NEVER changed: We will do all we can in one year time frame (actually 15 months) to affect the development of a successor venue to Key Arena. If we are unsuccessful at the end of the time frame, October 31, 2007, we will then evaluate our options. I have never wavered and will not."

His words conveyed the sentiment of an honest effort to keep the team in Seattle. The problem is that four months earlier, Bennet had said something that directly contradicts his assurances to David Stern. Tom Ward had emailed Bennett asking if there was "any way to move here for next season or are we doomed to have another lame-duck season in Seattle?"

Bennet replied, "I am a man possessed! Will do everything we can. Thanks for hanging with me boys, the game is getting started!"

Ward: "That's the spirit!! I am willing to help any way I can to watch ball here (in Oklahoma City) next year."

McClendon: "Me too, thanks Clay!" [2]

Those emails came during the one-year grace period supposedly earmarked for good-faith efforts to keep the team in Seattle. While Bennet publicly tried to keep the team in Seattle, his own emails show that he had been planning the exit the entire time. It sure seems like Bennet had lied. He had not been misleading or misrepresenting. He didn't just gloss over something. It seems he was flat out lying and Seattle had lost their team.

Seattle did not give up. In 2012, a group of investors came forward with a plan to build a new arena in Seattle's SoDo neighborhood. The investors hoped to revive the SuperSonics name and archives. On October 15, 2012, the King County Council voted unanimously in favor, while the Seattle City Council voted 7-2 to approve the amended SoDo multipurpose arena proposal. This led to the series of events that brought in Chris Hansen and the attempted purchase of the Kings.

In the time since losing the SuperSonics, many Seattle fans have cried foul, been outraged and called for legal action. They believe they had their team stolen from them and they may have a point, but being lied to was not the full reason they lost their team. They lost their team because they did not generate enough support for Howard Schutlz and his people, which led them to sell the team. They lost their team because so many of their fans were ready to let them go. They lost their team because they elected officials that said absurd things like, "The players should pay for the arena." They lost their team because from 1999-2008, the Seattle SuperSonics had a poor record on the court and attendance at the Key Arena was at an all-time low. You could argue that the fans did not support them because they were a bad organization that didn't deserve their support and you might be right. Regardless, there are plenty of other cities in the league with worse ownership, worse arenas and worse teams. Those cities have supported their teams enough to ensure they always have a team to support. In the end, the truth is that the city of Seattle and its fans did not do enough to keep their team, which leads to the story of what Sacramento and its fans did to keep their team.

It is important to understand a few things about the city of Sacramento. There is no other entertainment option in Sacramento. Sacramento is home to Oakland A's Triple-A team, the Rivercats, but even that is technically in West Sacramento. In Sacramento proper, there is little. Maybe tourists get a kick out of the capital building (or maybe not), but to people who live here, it is no big deal. There is the American River, which runs through much of the city and many surrounding areas. It provides many opportunities for recreation, biking and water activities. That said, the reality is that the Kings are all we have.

They are a financial boon to the economy. The Kings play at least 41 home games a year. That is at least 41 times a year that the city rocks. 41 times that downtown businesses do well and keep our economy spinning. When you start to account for all the events that no longer come to Sacramento, you are talking about many more days and nights of a booming downtown that we have been missing out on as well. Most major concert tours and artists now skip Sacramento. A few years ago, the NCAA tournament stopped coming here because they deemed the arena unfit. With no arena there would be no need for new hotels, new tourism, new investments in the city. Countless jobs would be lost and many more would never be created.

*A view of the Capital Building from across the street,
near where the new arena will be built.*

The current building is a disaster. From terrible acoustics to having one kitchen to make all of the food for 17,000 fans (most modern arenas have at least three), two loading docks (which is three fewer than most arenas have), an outdated ice rink (which runs on an ammonia-based freezing system that is all but obsolete), an ice rink configuration that was constructed perpendicularly to the basketball court, taking at least 15 hours to set up (most arenas make the switch in three hours and can have both a basketball game and a hockey game in one day), seats crammed too closely together and poor lighting in the completely inefficient parking lot. *Aside from that, the place is great.*

It is also the oldest non-renovated arena in all of sports (not just the NBA). It is antiquated beyond belief. Most people in this town do not realize how bad it is. If we could all see some of the other arenas in the NBA, I think people would understand what a bad place we have been in for years and the outcry for a new building would have been even louder. A new building brings the draw of sporting events, concerts and so much more. Not to mention, all this time the Kings have been playing outside of the city. ARCO Arena is in Natomas, not exactly the heart of Sacramento. When the new arena opens in downtown the city will change forever.

From there, the people will take over. The passion of Kings fans truly makes us one of the greatest fan bases in the world. When the Kings play, nothing else matters here. Bars and restaurants boom, people come out, and downtown becomes a place worth being. As I've said: this is much bigger than basketball. The

Kings are Sacramento's identity. There is no NFL, NHL or MLB team in Sacramento. For us, it's the Kings or nothing.

And when the team is winning, everyone is watching or listening.

I remember being stuck in my car during rush hour traffic while the Kings played a playoff game in 2002. The Sacramento heat was killing me (as usual). I was listening to the game on the radio as I sat stuck in my tiny red Toyota Tercel. With the freeway close to gridlock, I rolled down my window to get some air. As I did, I heard all the other car radios that were stuck on the freeway listening to the Kings game as well. It was one of the most awesome things I have ever experienced. It's beyond explanation.

That is what happens in this town. The place that Phil Jackson famously called a "cow town" truly loves basketball. More so than most people can ever understand. The voices of the Kings are known by almost everyone. People like Gary Gerould, Jerry Reynolds and Grant Napear are household names here. For the Kings to leave would have been a crushing blow to the people of this city and to its economy.

Then there is the story of Carmichael Dave, the local symbol and leader of the grassroots movements that would help save the Kings. Dave was a fan and who called into local sports radio shows for years and parlayed that into getting his own show. Dave is truly the leader of the Kings' people and voice of the fans. It started with a simple tweet after word came out that the Maloofs would try to move the team to Anaheim. Dave tweeted, "How much would you give to keep the Kings?" From there he said, "Wouldn't it be great if we could just bypass all the bureaucratic, red-tape-filled politicians in this city and have the Kings fans and city fans, because it's not just about the Kings, what if we could 'pass the hat' like in a church and build this thing on our own and come up with the money and tell all the politicians to get bent?"

And with that, Dave had given birth to more than three years of intense fan support. He then partnered with Jiffy Lube director of marketing Matt Graham to put the #HereWeBuild hashtag on electronic billboards all over Sacramento. When Mayor Johnson and Sacramento's business community convinced the NBA to give them another year to organize a funding plan, the public relations effort wasn't needed anymore. Dave wasn't done. He turned the "Here We Build" campaign into the "Here We Buy" campaign. Together, Dave helped collect over $500,000 in promised pledges for future tickets. Dave has been a non-stop rally machine for keeping the Kings in Sacramento. The fans here are all in debt to him. He is an example to follow for keeping hope, finding ways to make a difference, and defending the Kings of Sacramento. His is the kind of voice Seattle was missing.

And when the time came to defend the Kings, time and time again, this city rose up, led by Mayor Johnson. Johnson found and assembled an ownership group that would keep the team in Sacramento. From there, more than 11,000 Kings fans pledged to purchase season tickets for the team, provided that the team stays in Sacramento. Then the Sacramento City Council came up with a plan for a downtown arena that included $258 million in public money, without asking residents for a tax increase. From there, the ownership group, the fan support and the arena plan became great enough to convince the NBA not to move the Kings. All of this came together in a little over three months and it was all driven by the fans.

The Sacramento fans are the reason we still have the Kings.

A BRIEF HISTORY OF THE KINGS

*E*very story has a beginning. In this case, it isn't easy to pinpoint that moment. For me, it started when the Kings arrived in Sacramento from Kansas City in 1985. The team originally played in ARCO Arena, formally called the Sacramento Sports Arena and then called ARCO Arena I to distinguish it from its successor. At the time, it was one of the leagues smallest arenas, with a maximum capacity of just 10,333 people. It was supposed to be a first-stop for the Kings before a more suitable arena could be built. ARCO 1, as I always called it, was situated north of Sacramento's downtown, and was nicknamed by some "The Madhouse on Market Street." Every Kings game played in this venue was sold out. The building is also important for historical purposes, as the official name of "ARCO Arena" is the first known example of an NBA team selling naming rights to a brand new facility.

The Kings left ARCO 1 in 1988, moving to the new ARCO Arena, which was built one mile to the west. ARCO 1 survived as an office building for Sprint Communications for many years. On December 19, 2005, the California Department of Consumer Affairs moved their headquarters to that site. The place that was once built for the Kings still stands as office space.

In researching this book I made a trip out to Market Street to get a look at the old arena. I hadn't been there in almost 25 years. I got giddy seeing the place again, seeing this historical mark of Sacramento. This is one of the great symbols of what the people of Sacramento are capable of. A couple of state employees that saw me taking pictures thought I was crazy to care about this building that they called, "a mess."

ARCO 2, as it was known for a time, became, and still is, the home of the Kings. 25 years is a decent run for an arena, but eventually this building would come to be a huge problem.

In April of 1992, a group of Los Angeles developers, led by Jim Thomas, completed its $140 million purchase of the majority interest in the Sacramento Kings and Arco Arena. Thomas owned and ran the team for several years, during which time the Kings, on the court, enjoyed little to no success.

In 1996, Thomas began the process that would eventually lead to a new arena nearly 20 years later. That year Thomas proposed a huge and unrealistic downtown sports and entertainment complex that would be anchored by a major league baseball stadium and a new arena for his basketball team. It took Thomas two months to realize his dream would never happen in Sacramento and he dismissed the idea. Sacramento would likely never be home to multiple sports franchises and was not ready for such grand fantasies. The city lacked the ambition, resources or interest to work with Thomas on something so big. Instead, Thomas started working on a way out. He began talk of selling the team. The city responded by approving a $70 million loan to help refinance Arco Arena in 1997. Thomas backed off on his threat to sell the team, but that did not last long. It was clear that by this time, Thomas was completely done and ready to move on from Sacramento (a sentiment his successors would eventually feel about 14 years later).

On January 15, 1999, the Kings announced that Thomas had sold the team to the Maloof family from Albuquerque, N.M.

The Maloofs assumed controlling interest of Capital Sports and Entertainment, the organization that includes the Kings franchise and Arco Arena in the summer of 1999.

THE GREATEST SHOW ON COURT

The Maloofs' acquisition of the team coincided with the first and greatest era of success on the court for the Kings. In a period of three years, the team acquired starters Vlade Divac, Chris Webber, Peja Stojakovic, Doug Christie and Jason Williams (along with fan favorites like Jon Barry and Scott Pollard, who formed the "bench mob"). In 1999, Kings General Manager Geoff Petrie would win the executive of the year for assembling this group. These players, combined with the coaching of Rick Adelman and the Princeton offense, took the league by storm (Appendix 4). They ushered in a new era of basketball to Sacramento and to the NBA. They passed the ball as a team better than anyone before them and played a style that is now played by most teams in the league. They did special things together. (Appendix 5) In their first season together they made the playoffs, losing in the first round in five games to the formidable Utah Jazz led by John Stockton and Karl Malone. The following year, the team made the playoffs again and lost to the mighty Los Angeles Lakers.

In their third season under the Maloofs' ownership, the team made big headlines. For one, they made it to the second round of the playoffs, again losing to the Kobe-Shaq Lakers. During the season the team officially became the talk of the league, landing their starting five on the cover of *Sports Illustrated* with the headline, "The Greatest Show on Court." The Kings had officially arrived. After the season the team traded Jason Williams to Memphis for Mike Bibby. He, along with the other four, made up the core of the team that would contend for a title. The following season the team took the next step, making it to the Conference Finals. They went on to lose that series to the Lakers in seven games in a series that was allegedly fixed by NBA referees. Documents later revealed that at least one referee had taken money to affect games six and seven in the series. (Appendix 6)

While controversy about the series and the loss rained through the press, including presidential candidate Ralph Nader writing an open letter to the NBA calling for a fair playing field, actions off the court started to intensify.

On November 12, 2002, the Sacramento City Council agreed to join the Sacramento Kings and Union Pacific Railroad in a $654,000 consultant study on the merits of building a downtown basketball arena. This was a monumental moment for many reasons. For starters, it was a symbol of acknowledgment by the city that ARCO Arena would eventually need to be replaced. What Jim Thomas had tried to bully the city into doing six years earlier, they had begun the process of doing on their own. At this time, the Maloof family began to gain faith that the city might eventually do for them what they had never truly considered for Thomas.

In 2003, a consultant's report showed that the public would pay for the bulk of the costs for a proposed arena, with surcharges on things like restaurant food and beverages. The public at large did not take to this at all. People began to think twice about the process and started doubting the whole situation. *To be fair, the first couple arena plans the Maloofs presented were ridiculous.*

They were overly and unnecessarily extravagant and seemed more like palaces for the Maloofs than for the team and fans.

A year later, things began to sour. In May of 2004, Sacramento Mayor Heather Fargo recommended a plan that would put an arena in downtown Sacramento. Two months later, she backed off of the plan. Still, in August of that year, the Maloof family attended a City Council meeting to discuss the possibility of partnering to build the new arena. At this point, the Maloofs were operating in good faith with Fargo and the city. At this point, there was hope.

I truly believed that the Maloofs wanted to stay in Sacramento and that the city eventually forced their actions years later. I defended them for much longer than most other people. I gave them the benefit of the doubt for much longer than they deserved.

This meeting became famous for all the wrong reasons. Instead of an open discussion, the meeting quickly became one of demands and unreasonable behavior and speech. The city quickly announced to the Maloofs that they would cap their investment at $175 million. The Maloofs were stunned and got up and left the meeting. While it was not appropriate for them to do so, their reasoning made sense. When Fargo and the city chose to begin the meeting with their statement (which was really an ultimatum, and an unreasonable one at that) she showed her true motives. The truth is that Heather Fargo never wanted to build an arena, with or without any taxpayer money. She did not believe in using city funds to help the rich get richer. It is possible that she was initially open to it, but then changed

her mind when she saw the Maloofs original arena plans. In
any case, Fargo had no interest in helping the Maloofs, even
if it jeopardized the Kings' future in Sacramento. She did not
believe in the value that a professional franchise brought to
a city, did not understand the potential good it could do and
instead focused on other things.

With the Maloofs offended by the city and Fargo unwilling to
discuss the arena further, a series of failed attempts to build an
arena ensued. In 2004, Sheriff Lou Blanas released his plan to
pay for an arena with no taxpayer money. He worked for four
months with community leaders and landowners in an effort to
assemble private financing for a new arena. In February of 2005,
they concluded they could not raise enough money and gave up
the project.

On the court that season, the Kings' time as a serious
championship contender officially ended, signaled by the trade
of Chris Webber to the Philadelphia 76ers. Webber had hurt
his knee and never recovered, and the rest of the team had
aged. One year later, the Kings would make their last playoff
appearance.

In November of 2005, a local developer named Angelo K.
Tsakopoulos offered a new arena proposal to the Kings that
involved rezoning agricultural land for development and using
the profits to build an arena for the basketball team.

In March of 2006, Thomas Enterprises submitted a new arena
plan that included high-rise housing along the river, a 1,000-seat

live theater and a new sports arena anchoring an entertainment district.

This is where the story takes a twist.

In 2006, the city finally appeared to be ready to play ball with the NBA and the Maloofs. They acknowledged that a new arena needed to be built and placed the now infamous measures Q and R on the ballot. Q and R called for a quarter-of-a-cent sales tax increase that could be used to help fund the construction of an arena. It would have appeased the Maloofs, the NBA and everyone else. Everyone could have still won if these two measures passed. The city would get a quarter-cent tax but they would get to keep the Kings. Unfortunately, this project was doomed to fail.

A big press conference was called to rally support for the initiatives. City leaders would speak. The Maloofs would tell the fans to get behind the measures. Hope was blooming everywhere. Everything in the universe had been aligned for this. The press conference was going very well and everyone was excited until Joe Maloof took the stage and completely torpedoed any hope of the measures passing.

Instead of the talking points he had received from the city, he chose to read from a script written by Maloof family attorneys. He stumbled through the speech and buried the deal in epic fashion. Instead of praising the plan and calling on the fans, he went another direction. He questioned the viability of the site and the parking situation. At the same time, he also said that if the measures didn't pass, the Maloofs would have to consider other cities. He was saying, "it's not a good deal, but if you don't do it we might leave." He undermined all faith in the project and that led to the measures failing miserably, with only 20 percent of voters voting in favor. He had crushed the city, the fans, and (probably) any hope of the city ever working with the Maloofs again.

In September of 2006, the Maloofs announced that they had abandoned talks with the city and county of Sacramento over the terms of locating a new arena in the downtown rail yard.

Then in October of 2006, the Maloof brothers appeared in an infamous Carl's Jr. advertisement in which they offer a combo of burger, fries and a $6000 bottle of wine. While the Maloofs said it was just a commercial, they began to signal their ignorance of the situation. Commercial or not, they depicted themselves as super-rich billionaires at the same time they were asking taxpayers to build them a new arena. The people of Sacramento noticed and, frankly, most turned on them. The majority of people here no longer wanted anything to do with the Maloofs, some so much so that they would have been happy to see them go even if it meant losing the Kings.

Later in 2006, with the relationship between the city and team in a free-fall, NBA commissioner David Stern arrived in Sacramento to help lead a new arena effort. He brought in NBA arena consultant John Morag to fact-find and see what he could do to help. Meanwhile, the team was in limbo. With the

Maloofs no longer committed to the franchise, they began to slash salaries and the team on the court became one of the worst in the league.

K.J. TO THE RESCUE

*A*fter three years in limbo, on January 14, 2010, the NBA announced it was backing a land-swap proposal that would move the California State Fair to the Arco Arena site in Natomas and build a new arena and entertainment complex next to the downtown train depot. In March, the city announced they were open to exploring the plan, which was called the, "Sacramento Convergence Plan." The NBA usually gets what it wants, and at the time, it wanted this plan to work. But like all the arena plans before it, this plan was also doomed for failure. The failure of measures Q and R just three years prior made it obvious that the public would never vote in favor of any tax increase, and without a huge amount of public money the Convergence Plan never stood a chance. Later that year, Cal Expo officials strongly rejected the plan. Four days later the NBA announced that they would no longer take an active role in arena efforts. Just like that, the plan was dead. Hope was low. Little did we realize that something had happened two years earlier that would give us one last chance to keep the Kings: we had elected Kevin Johnson as mayor.

This would not have been a great place for an arena anyway.

In January of 2011, the city, led by Mayor Johnson, began working with developer David Taylor to examine the feasibility of a new arena in the downtown rail yards. At the same time, the Maloofs had already begun plans to move the team out of Sacramento. In February of 2011, Commissioner Stern confirmed that the Maloofs were in talks with the City of Anaheim. Meanwhile, Anaheim put together a $75 million dollar incentive for the Kings to move to Anaheim. With the Maloofs ready to leave town and the city grasping at their last straws to save the team, the stage was set for an April 14th meeting at the league offices in New York. There, the Maloofs would present their case to the other owners for moving the Kings to Anaheim. Kevin Johnson would be allowed to present his defense for keeping the Kings in Sacramento. Hope in Sacramento was at an all-time low. Based on the series of prior events, it seemed likely that we would lose the Kings. We had failed time and again to generate the kind of public support (and money) needed to build an arena. The owners of our team had tried for years to get an arena built to keep the Kings here and we had not been up to the challenge. The Maloofs had gone quiet in the press and stopped attending Kings games. Worst of all, the Maloofs had another city ready to provide them with what they needed. The Maloofs expected little resistance to their plan to move. They thought their team would be playing in Anaheim in time for the following season. Kevin Johnson had other plans.

The day of the meeting came and Kevin Johnson shocked the world. Johnson showed up to the meetings with the backing of supermarket tycoon Ronald Burkle and presented an offer to the league in which Ron Burkle, in partnership with lobbyist and developer Darius Anderson, would purchase the Kings or buy another team for the city should the Kings move to Anaheim. Johnson had pulled a rabbit out of his hat that the league had to consider. Getting billionaire Burkle on board helped Johnson show the league and the world that there were legitimate businessmen who believed the Kings could thrive in Sacramento. Burkle was the money that proved Johnson's statements. The Maloof family left the meetings outraged. It turns out that about one month earlier, Burkle had called the Maloofs and asked if there was anything he could do to help and was refused by the Maloofs. Johnson had sensed Burkle's interest and recruited him to help save the Kings. The Maloofs had showed up expecting to get what they wanted, but instead had been surprised and out-played by Kevin Johnson. The next day the NBA extended the deadline for a Kings decision to May 2.

The Maloofs had a short period of time to regroup and try to put together another plan or to do something else. They failed to do so and when May 2nd came they announced that the Kings would stay in Sacramento and that they would do their part to secure a plan for the desperately needed sports arena. The truth is that they thought they had found a golden parachute in Anaheim, that they had it in their hands, then had it snatched away from them. Having no other choice, they began to say some of the right things and appeared resigned to giving Sacramento another chance (but only because they had to).

Joe Maloof went on the radio the next day and posed the question to listeners, "what would you do if you were in our situation?"

What he meant was, "if you owned a team and needed a new arena, worked with the city for years and got nowhere, wouldn't you be looking to move too?" He might have even had a point. If you have a business in one location losing money and you know that you can start making money again if you move the business somewhere else, no matter how much you love the first location, you have to consider moving. This was the truth and it made some sense. The problem is that the Maloofs had already turned people off. His question came off as hostile. Instead of gaining sympathy he, once again, made himself the ire of many Kings fans' anger. Worse, the Kings would remain in limbo.

That season I went to the Kings second-to-last home game of the year with my dad. We were braced for the fact that it might be the very last Kings game we would ever go to. Looking back, I can see now that the odds of the Maloofs successfully moving the Kings to Anaheim were not very good. Despite the severity of the Maloof threats, the truth is that the NBA did not want or need a team in Anaheim. Lakers' owner Jerry Buss was also known to be strongly against the move. It would have been very hard for the league to accept Anaheim. Kevin Johnson had made it much easier for the league to deny the move.

The Maloof family went public again, saying they would give the city one more shot to get a new arena built. Once again, the NBA sent a group to investigate what had gone wrong. The Maloofs turned all of the negotiations for a new arena over to the NBA and their group. What had really gone wrong is that Sacramento was finally in a position where they were willing and able to help the Maloofs keep the team in Sacramento at a time when the Maloofs were exasperated and sick of working with them.

The city moved forward, slowly but surely, with efforts to build a sports and entertainment facility. In May of 2011, developer David Taylor and ICON Venue Group issued an analysis describing a new arena and entertainment facility in downtown Sacramento that would cost $387 million, would fit on city-owned land near Fifth and H streets and would be open by 2015. Also in May of 2011, Mayor Johnson announced he would form a 60-member commission made up of elected leaders and business and labor representatives from across the region to come up with a plan to finance a new arena.

Later in 2011, Johnson's Think Big Sacramento task force proposed a group of possible arena funding options. The options included ticket surcharges, private investments, the sale of city-owned land and, just maybe, privatization of city parking.

The idea was simple. At night in downtown Sacramento, over 10,000 parking spots that are filled during the day (mostly by state employees) sit empty. What if those spots were filled and being paid for by people using a downtown arena, who would need places to park anyway? This solution not only found a source for arena funding, but one that would generate those funds on its own. It would not divert funds from other public needs like police, schools and the like. If there was no arena, there would be no people needing to park, so the money the parking spots generate would be new money.

In December of 2011, the Sacramento City Council voted 7-2 to ask companies interested in leasing the city's downtown parking operations to step forward. Then in February 2012, the council allowed their staff to enter negotiations with 11 different firms with interest in leasing the downtown parking.

Incredibly, Johnson had found a solution to the biggest problem of all: the public contribution. Knowing that no ballot measure or tax would ever pass in the current recession, he had found a mechanism for public funding of an arena that would not require a ballot initiative and would not take money away from other projects. In fact, it will continue to generate new money, along with thousands of jobs for the next three years and then hundreds per year after that.

This has been a huge point of contention for many in Sacramento who think that the city should not be spending money on an arena and instead focus on the other needs of the city. To the last remaining people in Sacramento who still object, let it be clear: the money that the city will be contributing to the arena is not money that would be taken away from other things. It is not going to make our streets less safe or put fewer doctors in hospitals. It is not going to cause our schools to have fewer teachers and fewer resources. It is coming from new money, a new source of value that the city realized it had: night-time parking spaces. It's coming from the hundreds of nights that people will be spending money in downtown and needing somewhere to park. That, combined with a huge investment in our city from outsiders. The kind of outside investment that no other business could generate for the city. Having a team here is an amazing thing for the local economy and privatization of local parking is the single biggest thing that changed and stopped the team from moving. (Appendix 7)

With a public funding mechanism finally discovered and approved, there was truly hope for the first time that Sacramento could get an arena built for the Kings. The question became, "Was it too late?"

On February 27, 2012 the question was answered. Sacramento officials and the Kings agreed to a $387 million plan created by NBA officials in which the city would shoulder more than half the cost of a new arena and own the facility. The Maloofs would put in $75 million up front and provide the city with another $75 million in arena-related revenue over 30 years. On March 6, 2012, by a 7-2 vote, the Sacramento City Council approved the financing plan for a downtown sports arena now costing $391 million.

Sacramento Kings representatives and the Maloof family agreed to the deal during a negotiation session at All-Star Weekend in Orlando. The Kings were finally going to stay in Sacramento. During the next Kings home game, there was a celebration with Joe and Gavin Maloof standing hand in hand with Kevin Johnson. Speeches were made and everyone was happy. Gavin declared, "There is going to be a beacon of light shining bright in 2015, a brand new arena!"

I was there. The words he said seemed true, but he did not feel honest.

This is the very last time Sacramento fans would cheer for any member of the Maloof family ever again. Behind the scenes, the wheels were already in motion. The Maloofs backed out of the deal a couple of weeks later. From this point forward the Maloofs would not even try to hide their disdain for Sacramento. They didn't have to speak with the city anymore to tell them where they stood. The Maloofs had decided that the deal wasn't good enough and they were done negotiating with Sacramento. They wanted out.

FOURTH QUARTER

With the NBA Board of Governors still in session, George Maloof held an impromptu press conference. The Maloofs had previously killed a deal in one statement in 2006. In 2012, they would kill all deals once and for all. It turns out that George was there to scuttle the deal. With cameras rolling, he turned the microphone over to an economist to explain how Sacramento couldn't afford the deal. The room stood still in shock. The Maloofs instead suggested a plan to renovate the existing ARCO Arena. This was a slap in the face and made no sense, as years of studies had concluded that renovation of the building would cost more than a new building. The Maloofs didn't like the deal and were looking for a way to explain themselves. In the process, they had gone too far.

Commissioner Stern had spent months putting the deal together only to see the Maloofs blow it at the last minute. Stern tried to give the Maloofs one last chance to do the deal. He offered to have the league loan them their share of the money needed for the arena project (on top of the money the league had already loaned them) in order to facilitate the deal. Stern wanted this to happen. Still, the Maloofs said no to Sacramento and Stern.

The Maloofs had been involved in bad business before, but this time they had gone too far. This time, they had crossed David Stern. Stern was quoted as saying, "In my view, it was always subject to any party saying they didn't want to do it. It was always non-binding and I think it's fair for the Maloofs to say they don't want to do it. If they had done that a little simpler, a little earlier and a little more directly, it could have saved a lot of angst and trouble." [3]

That was Stern's way of being political. What he was really saying was, "Look you idiots, we have been playing these games and doing these dances in Sacramento for 15 years and I'm sick of it. I am retiring in two years and having another small-market team relocate after all we've done would be a disaster for my legacy. I am giving you a way out of your situation and you won't take it. This is not ok. You will not cross me again." (Appendix 8)

Mayor Johnson finally publicly criticized the Maloofs as well. At a press conference he said, "They are now saying they don't want to do the deal, which essentially means they don't want to be in Sacramento. I think Sacramento deserves a partner that would honor their commitment. I think Sacramento deserves a partner who wants to work in good faith. And I think Sacramento deserves better than what we've gotten up to this point."

The Maloofs had been bad business partners and neither the NBA nor the City of Sacramento wished to continue working with them. Whatever goodwill the people of Sacramento still had for the Maloofs was now completely gone and their image in Sacramento was ruined. In any case, there was still an arena deal backed by the city and the league. Unfortunately, the Maloofs still owned the team and they were not in the mood to sell. Johnson still had potential buyers in people like Ron Burkle and other Silicon Valley players. Still, at no point did the Maloofs ever acknowledge that the team was for sale or field any offers from local buyers, even ones who could give them the kind of money they wanted.

Instead, they spent the next year flirting with Virginia Beach and looking for other cities and buyers.

Virginia Beach and other cities were never realistic, only Seattle could help the Maloofs now.

Eventually they would meet Chris Hanson, who was working with the city of Seattle. While the NBA had said no to the Maloofs before, Seattle had something special going for it. Seattle was the place that had previously had a team taken away from it. What if David Stern felt like making amends to a city he had disowned before? What if someone could offer so much money that the league would have to consider it? The Maloofs believed that with Hanson's bottomless pockets and Seattle's sympathy factor, they could get out of Sacramento once and for all. On January 13, 2013, the Maloofs (illegally) signed a binding agreement with the Hansen-Ballmer Group to sell their share of the Kings at a valuation of $525 million. That would place the Maloofs' take at approximately $341 million for 65 percent of the franchise, with 53 percent for the Maloofs and 12 percent for minority owner Bob Hernreich. On February 5th, David Stern announced that the Hansen-Ballmer Group had officially filed to move the Kings to Seattle.

While the Maloofs looked to Seattle, Kevin Johnson looked two hours south of Sacramento to Silicon Valley, computer capital of the universe and all the wealth it brings. There, he found Vivek Ranadive and convinced him to join the effort. To appreciate the significance, a little about the new Kings' owner: Vivek Ranadive is an incredibly successful Indian businessman, engineer, author, and philanthropist. He grew up in the Juhu area of Bombay, India and was the youngest of three children. After arriving in the United States with $50 to his name, he went on to build an empire. He founded and was CEO of TIBCO, a billion dollar computer company. He is also credited with digitizing Wall Street in the 1980s with his first company, Teknekron Software Systems. Ranadive came from nothing to accomplish everything. Unlike the Maloofs, he has a personal record of great success in business. He is a role model for many.

Whatever Johnson said or did, he landed the biggest and last whale he needed by convincing Ranadive to join him. While he worked on finding whales in the Bay Area, he also recruited Mark Mastrov, the founder of the 24 Hour Fitness chain, and Dale Carlsen of Sleep Train Mattress Centers to join a potential venture. Ron Burkle had to step out on April 8th because he was in talks with Relativity Media to launch Relativity Sports, an agency that intends to represent athletes, coaches and broadcasters. By rule, Burkle's involvement in the venture would complicate his ability to serve as a financial partner in any purchase of an NBA franchise, including the Kings. Burkle remains in discussions to be a part of the team re-building downtown Sacramento, but not as a buyer for the team.

On March 8th, David Stern told the media that there was "substantial variance" between the offers put forth by groups from Seattle and Sacramento, and that the latter bid would have to improve if the Kings were to stay put.

On April 12th, the Seattle group upped its valuation of the Kings from $525 million to $550, which meant that that the Hansen-Ballmer consortium would pay the Maloofs an additional $16 million for their controlling stake in the team, putting the price tag at $357 million total.

It was time for all parties involved to dance one last time. With the yearly owners meetings coming, once again it was up to Kevin Johnson to stop the Maloofs and save the Kings. Early in 2013, Johnson announced he had been granted an audience with the NBA board of governors to present a competing bid that would prevent the Maloofs from selling the Kings to the group from Seattle. Johnson had fought the Maloofs to a draw twice before. This time, one way or another, it would end. Either the Maloofs would take the team away to Seattle with them, or they would finally have to consider selling to investors who would keep the team in Sacramento.

On Monday, April 30th, Johnson struck a major victory for Sacramento when the league announced that an NBA ownership committee studying the situation unanimously voted against relocating the Kings. The announcement was huge, but the battle was not completely over. Still, moments after the announcement, Johnson tweeted, "That's what I'm talking about SACRAMENTO!!!!! WE DID IT!!!!! I've never been prouder of this city. I thank the ownership group, city leaders, but most of all the BEST FANS IN THE NBA!!!"

The decision was a blow to Seattle, but Hanson vowed to move forward with the transaction he had signed with the Maloof family to buy and move the franchise anyway. In fact, Hanson still had one last trick up his sleeve. Desperate to persuade the NBA to change their mind, Hanson increased his offer just days before the NBA was scheduled to vote on relocation. Hanson's latest bid put a value on the Kings at $625 million. This was an increase of $75 million over his previous offer. It was an offer that would put the team value on par with that of the most expensive teams in the NBA. The offer was also $100 million above what was being offered by Johnson, Ranadive and the local investors. To further sweeten the pot, Hanson also offered each NBA team a relocation fee payout of more than $4 million, a total of $115 million, in hopes of securing the 16 votes Seattle needed for the original sale agreement to be ratified.

The Maloofs were not done, either. They threatened to retain ownership of the Kings if the team's relocation to Seattle wasn't approved. On top of that, the Maloofs put together a backup agreement in which they would sell 20 percent of the team to the Hansen-Ballmer group for $125 million in order to allow the incumbent owners to continue operating the organization. This would be a set up for Hanson to fail to build an arena in Sacramento and eventually move the team to Seattle.

In response to the news, the NBA called an emergency meeting scheduled for the day before the league was scheduled to officially vote on the matter. For a couple of days, fans in Seattle and Sacramento held their breath. In Sacramento, we feared the worst. We feared that we had done what we had to do, but that perhaps the money Hanson was offering was just too much for the league to pass up. Perhaps Hanson and his money would win the day.

On Wednesday, May 15th Hansen and Seattle took their final blow. The league's 30 owners killed the 5-month-old deal between Hanson and the Maloofs. After hours of presentations, speeches and debating, a 22-8 vote against relocation meant that Hanson's dream was over. The NBA board of governors ruled that Sacramento's last-minute push to put together a buyer's group, draw up an arena financing plan and win City Council approval was more than enough for the city to keep the team. The last step would be to get the Maloofs to agree to a deal with the Ranadive group.

Theoretically, the Maloofs could have held on to the team, continued to have them as a lame duck and eventually tried to force the league to help them through legal action. Fortunately for everyone, the Maloofs were done fighting. With the league voting emphatically against relocation they knew that their dreams were over and it was time to cut a deal and move on. The next day they reached an agreement to sell to the Ranadive group. The deal was made official the following day. The league had already given the okay on the deal, as it was the same deal they had created and agreed to with the Maloofs in 2012. Vivek Ranadive had come to an agreement to purchase 65 percent of the Kings from the Maloof family for approximately $348 million. The Sacramento ownership group also included 24 Hour Fitness founder Mark Mastrov, former Facebook senior executive Chris Kelly and the Jacobs family, founders of communications giant Qualcomm. The Kings' total valuation in the sale is $535 million, an NBA record. The deal was a monumental symbol for the success of the NBA, as one of their least valued franchises had just been sold for more money than their most valued teams were previously worth. Despite turning down Hanson's money, the league had still gotten much richer (and did it without taking a team away from a city that deserved to have one).

The news in the coming days revealed that the Ranadive group had improved its chances of swaying the Maloofs at the 11th hour by agreeing to put 100 percent of the money it would owe the Maloofs into an escrow account. David Stern said the Ranadive group secured $240 million for their offer. That amount includes roughly $200 million to buy the franchise from the Maloofs that has been placed in an escrow account, plus a cushion of $40 million to operate the franchise. Ranadive also agreed to absorb a line of credit the Maloofs had with the NBA, as well as assume the payments of a $64 million loan owed to the City of Sacramento by the Kings franchise related to Sleep Train Arena (formerly Arco Arena). The value of those debts was removed from the amount that would be given to the Maloofs. After $60 million of debt owed to the City of Sacramento plus money owed to the NBA, the Maloofs are expected to clear a little more than $200 million from the sale. When they bought the team, they paid the valuation of $156 million. That is a decent gain for them (not accounting for inflation and other factors), but if they had been true to Sacramento and been good businessmen all along, they could have had much more. This city would have given the family what they wanted if they hadn't turned on it so many times.

In Sacramento, it was time to celebrate at last. Kevin Johnson announced to screaming Kings fans that the deal to sell the NBA franchise to the Ranadive group had been signed. The announcement at a City Hall rally brought to an end years of maneuvering by Johnson to secure a new ownership group, convinced the council to commit to building a new downtown arena, and showed the NBA that the capital city of the most populous state in the nation has the fan base to make the venture successful. Johnson said the plan for the Kings' future includes a $447 million downtown arena that will be built at the western gateway to the city near the Sacramento River.

Johnson said, "The fans – you never gave up, you never lost hope, you supported us. Every time we fell down, you picked us up and said, 'Keep fighting ... We can do it. Our voices will be heard. We will not be ignored.' The fans of Sacramento, this is your moment – truly, your moment. In terms of building a brand-new building, it's been very clear and we've said this time and time again: Building a building downtown is bigger than basketball. It's transformative. You're going to see a situation where Sacramento will be changed forever for the good because of what's transpired in the last couple days." He also took a moment to acknowledge Seattle and their efforts. "We wish Seattle the best. Great sports town, great ownership group, and Chris Hansen and Ballmer, and those folks, I hope they get a team at some point, I think they will. And this is just me, but I'm rooting for Seattle. If there is any way we can be helpful, you know, we will. They were awesome. Our hat goes off to them and their fans." [4]

He was right. Sacramento had been through so much over the years, nearly losing the Kings at least three times. It was finally time to celebrate. A rally the next week included speeches by Johnson and Ranadive, along with current and former Kings players, such as Chris Webber, Scott Pollard, Tyreke Evans and Isiah Thomas. An estimated crowd of more than 10,000 people filled the streets of downtown Sacramento to celebrate.

The voice of the Kings, Grant Napear, said it best (as he always does): "I think it's the best part of it – we all feel we accomplished something because everybody did something to save this team. The fans are unparalleled. A lot of fans would've jumped ship, a lot of fans would've given up, but this fan base never gave up. (During) the last game against the Clippers on April 17, if you'd walked in and didn't know any better, you would've sworn you were at a Playoff game. These fans and this community, I think they're a big reason why this team is staying here."

Napear was exactly right. For all the money issues, politics and big names that led to this final result, it was ultimately the fans that drove them. It was the Sacramento fans that pushed them as hard as possible to do the right thing: find a way to keep the Kings in Sacramento. Kevin Johnson and his people led the way and did their part, but it was the fans that made it happen.

Ranadive declared, "It's the start of a new era." For Sacramento, it is indeed.

As for Seattle, they begin another chapter of their own. Hansen released a statement saying, "While we are obviously extremely disappointed with today's relocation vote and truly believe we put forth both a significantly better offer and arena plan, we do thank the league and the owners for their time and consideration and look forward to hearing back on our agreement to join the Maloofs as limited partners in the Kings. But most of all I would like to thank everyone in Seattle who has been a part of our effort and supported our cause. Words simply can't express how much your support has meant to me personally and to our city. I truly believe we did everything possible to put our best foot forward in this process and you all should be proud and hold your heads high today. Our day will come ... and when it does it will just be that much sweeter for the struggle. I love you, Seattle!"

Adam Silver is the NBA executive who will become commissioner next year when Stern retires. He recently suggested Seattle may have a better shot now at an expansion team than previously thought. Silver said, "We have never wavered in our desire to return to the Seattle market at some point. Expansion was discussed (today), at least as a possibility down the road ... we fully expect to return (to Seattle) one day." [5]

Seattle's day will come, but for Sacramento, the time is now.

CONCLUSION

*W*hat the city, Kevin Johnson, and Vivek Randadive have done and will do is important on so many levels and affects so many people. I know; I lived through all these events and have the memories, joy and pain to show for it. (Appendix 9)

Kevin Johnson and the city of Sacramento have gotten Ranadive and his friends to do amazing things with us already.

I am sure that when Ranadive made the decision to purchase the Kings he knew many things. He knew that he was buying an NBA franchise with perhaps the most devoted fans in the world and, because of that, he knew that he was making a great investment financially, ethically and socially. The man is a philanthropist and this gives him another opportunity shape how he and his family will be perceived. He is giving himself a new toy and a new passion. He knows this is an amazing opportunity for himself and others. He will have a chance to shape the future of a city.

I believe Ranadive has an idea of how important he has become to this city and its people, but I also doubt he understands all the ramifications of his actions. I doubt he understands that he is truly, *Saving Sacramento*.

APPENDICES

APPENDIX 1
JASON COLDIRON THE FAN

I have lived in Sacramento for 35 years and loved the Kings since they got here, 28 years ago. I have watched the city and surrounding areas be built. I have watched the city develop. I have memories of people and events. I see the major buildings and restaurants and remember long ago when they weren't even there. I grew up here. I know this town and I know this team. This is a city that loves the Kings and I am just one of many. I have not been the loudest or most die-hard Kings fan in this town. There are thousands here who have bled purple and turned this place into the beacon of fan enthusiasm that it has become. People who can remember know: when there is any kind of effort on the court (there doesn't even have to be success), this place is the loudest in the NBA. The cowbells rock, the feet stomp and the voices scream. How loud do Sacramento Kings fans get? During the playoffs against the Lakers in 2002 the decibel level was measured as high as 112, about the same as a jet engine. Given a new facility and competent ownership, this place will already start to rock in 2013. The real party will come in the fall of 2016 when the new arena opens in time for the 2016 Kings season. This town is going to be something else. Even people who know don't fully understand what is happening here. Even the skeptics will come to understand. They will party with all those who love the Kings and helped the grand achievement of getting them stay here. And somehow, some way, I will be there.

APPENDIX 2
THE MALOOFS' BEHAVIOR

*T*he Maloofs didn't really hate Sacramento. They hated the situation they were in. They hated that they were stuck in a place where they believed they could no longer make money.

And they hated that the City of Sacramento, the NBA and the world at large was out to get them. I still don't understand these people. I have a degree in Psychology and have been studying the Maloofs and their business for years and I still do not understand their behavior in Sacramento.

APPENDIX 3
THE LAST KINGS' PLAYOFFS

In the 05-06 playoffs, the Kings faced the San Antonio Spurs in the first round. The team had a unique, physical style of play led by Ron Artest and Bonzi Wells. Bill Walton (the legendary commentator at the time) said that the Kings could beat the Spurs and that they were a dangerous team. The series featured highs and lows. The high was Kevin Martin's game-winning layup on a fast-break in game two that blew a hole in the roof of Arco with the noise the fans made. The lowlight was game four when the Kings had the game in hand in the final seconds and Mike Bibby mysteriously left Brent Barry open in the corner, who got the ball, made the three-pointer and won the game. The Spurs went on to win the series and the Kings have not been to the playoffs since.

Note: Mike Bibby was a heck of a player for the Kings. He never made an all-star team in his career but he was among the best offensive point guards in the NBA for many years. He always made the right decisions on the fast break and was an amazing shooter. Most importantly, he looked down the barrel of many, many critical shots in the Kings' playoff runs. When the game was on the line (and Chris Webber was avoiding making eye contact with him so he wouldn't get the ball), Bibby was the guy you wanted taking the shot. On the flip side, he is truly one of the worst defensive players I have ever seen. I would not feel comfortable trusting him to guard the chair I am sitting in right now. Ironically, that was basically his job on the play above and he failed it miserably. The situation in the game was simple; give up the two if you have to, but absolutely, positively do not leave Brent Barry open behind the three-point line. Instead, he jumped in to defend a driving Tim Duncan, who swung the ball around and Barry ended up with a wide open three. When they get beat by their man, NBA players are taught to call for help and rotate to another man. Even most guys at the local playgrounds and gyms know this. On this play, Mike Bibby did the same version of that he always did. His man got by him... and he stood there like a deer in headlights and didn't do anything, simply waiting helplessly for the play to end and to get the ball back.

RICK ADELMAN AND THE PRINCETON OFFENSE

One of the biggest keys to the Kings success was how Coach Rick Adelman and his assistants implemented the "Princeton" offense. Adelman brought on assistant coach Pete Carril (who is widely credited with perfecting the offense, although technically it can be traced all the way back to the 1930's when Franklin Cappon used it at Princeton) to help teach it to the players. Carril came to become one of the most beloved figures in Sacramento for players and fans alike. The Princeton offense is a strategy that emphasizes constant motion, passing, back-door cuts, picks on and off the ball, and disciplined teamwork. These would come to be hallmarks of Kings basketball. The offense is designed for a unit of five players who can each pass, shoot and dribble at an above average level. It attempts to isolate and exploit mismatches using these skills. Positions become less important and on offense, with no "point guard" designated on the floor. (Still, point guards like Mike Bibby and Jason Williams thrived in this offense.)

The offense is often considered a variation of the "triangle offense" that Phil Jackson won 11 championships with in Chicago and Los Angeles. That is a bit of a fallacy, since technically the Princeton offense was born first. Regardless, the similarities are there, especially as the styles pertain to point guards. Fundamentally, the main difference between the two offenses is that in the triangle, the pass that initiates the offense goes to a player in the post, with cuts and movement in each direction going around that player as the play develops, leading to all the mismatches and mix-ups the offense is designed to create. In Adelman's Princeton version, the initial pass is made to a player near the elbow or high post on one side of the key, allowing more room closer to the basket for cutters and, in the case of the Kings at the time, taking advantage of Webber and Divac's ability to make shots and pass anywhere from that spot, which extended defenses even further away from the basket, allowing even more cutting and weak-side action.

In their heyday, like clockwork, the Kings ran a play in the first quarter of every game that took advantage of everything that the Princeton offense is designed to do and what made them so darn good. Doug Christie would take the ball at the top of the three-point line straight on. Peja Stojakovic would run off of a series of screens on each side by Webber and Divac while Bibby or Williams drew attention in the corners. Stojakovic crossed under the hoop and ran off the screens as many times as necessary until he found an opening under the basket (which he inevitably always did), at which point Christie would zip a pass right through the middle of the defense for an easy score. With as much success as they had running this play, I always wondered why they only ran it once a game. What I eventually realized is that later in the game they ran the same play but with a guard other than Christie at the top, in order to create confusion at that point. Also, the fact that teams knew that early in the game Peja would be near the rim on the play meant that he would have more success getting open from long range (mind you at the time, he was arguably the very best shooter in the entire world).

General Manager Geoff Petrie did an amazing job building the perfect team to play this style. They had above-average passers and multi-skilled players at every position on the floor. Chris Webber and Vlade Divac were born to play in this offense and, since they were the first two players in this group to join the team, Adelman was able to build the offense around them.

Many Kings fans at the time bashed Webber constantly for not posting up enough. The truth is that the offense rarely called for him to do so. (Webber was flawed in many ways, but this was not one of them.)

APPENDIX 5
THE GREATEST SHOW ON COURT

*I*n a span of three years, a bad team was built into a contender. Under the leadership of Geoff Petrie and others, the team assembled their amazing group in a fashion that is the model for the NBA world: they added pieces through free-agency, from the draft, and through trades. They made progress in the playoffs for three consecutive years and would have won an NBA title if not for a couple of bad minutes and some bad officiating. A break here or there and we could have been talking about one of the greatest team success stories ever.

In 1998 the Maloofs took over the team, joining the league just in time for a strike that wiped out half of the 1998-99 season. All teams played just 50 games that season. There was no All-Star game that year. Michael Jordan had just retired from the Bulls, leaving the NBA looking for a new identity and new stars to celebrate. To top it all off, when negotiations finally ended, teams had very little time to get their acts together for the season. They scrambled to fill out their teams. The free-agency period that normally takes place over a couple of months was essentially packed into one week, with teams already starting to practice even without full rosters. It was a very unique time for the NBA and for the Kings, and one that shaped the league for the next few years. Perhaps it is fitting that the Maloofs got to start with a clean slate in Sacramento, just as the NBA as a whole was doing in many ways.

I listened to Greg Napear (the voice of the Kings) and others talk on the radio every day for three hours at that point in my life, mostly while I was at work. I got excited every day for months to hear what was going on with the Kings and how they would be re-built. I played NBA video games and practiced team-building. Combined with the infancy of espn.com and other sports sites, this was a very special time to be a fan.

Chris Webber had already been acquired from the Washington Bullets for Mitch Richmond, giving the Kings a legitimate superstar.

It turns out that Webber didn't want to be here at all. His father counseled him to give the city a chance and eventually he did, after some time when it seemed he might try to force a trade. I listened to Napear debate the subject with fans for months during the strike. Webber stayed and led the Kings to great things. The team never would have accomplished the amazing things it did without him. In a twist of bitter irony, they also never made it over the top and to a championship because of him.

The Kings scrambled (just as all the other teams did) and made an amazing series of signings. The headliner was getting Vlade Divac to come to the West Coast and give the Kings a legitimate, name-brand center. It was huge symbolically for the Kings, getting a player of his stature to actually want to come here. This made a big difference in the coming years as the team added pieces in building their contender. Two days after Divac, Webber reported to Sacramento and the Kings signed Jon Barry and an aging Vernon Maxwell, among others.

Barry later said that he showed up in Sacramento expecting to already be one of the main guys, only to find that he was one of six players competing for two spots. Fortunately, Barry lasted and became one of the greatest Kings ever.

The Kings' first round draft pick that year was an exciting point guard from the south named Jason Williams, who was about to set the town ablaze with his passing skills and make highlight reels every night for the next two years. They also added Predrag Stojakovic, whom they had drafted three years earlier and waited for him to come to the United States. Petrie had befriended and worked with Peja and his family for many years before drafting him and eventually convincing him to come to the United States. The story of how that happened is one of many great moves Petrie made back then.

The team had immediate success with the new group, but as the core was built gradually, the team also progressed gradually. In the strike-shortened season of 99', the team actually made it into the playoffs as the sixth seed in the Western Conference after going 27-23 in the regular season, mostly because they had gelled together much quicker than other teams under the difficult circumstances. The Kings led their first round series 2-1 before the Utah Jazz took the last two games in dramatic fashion. Game 5 came down to a last-second hook shot by Vlade Divac that missed, ending the Kings' surprising season. The city was starting the take basketball very seriously and didn't handle the loss well at all.

In Game 4, John Stockton had gone around a Karl Malone screen and stood wide open for what seemed like seven days before hitting the game-winner in the final moments of the game. The morning after, the pastor at my church called John Stockton, "a thief in the night" during his sermon.

After the season, the team traded Corliss Williamson to the Toronto Raptors for Doug Christie. Williamson had been a solid player since the Kings drafted him, but did not fit the style that they were now playing. The move gave the team one elite defender in Christie, who went on to make multiple All- NBA Defensive teams and provided the team with another kind of toughness that they would need to contend with the big boys. The move also allowed Stojakovic to move into the starting lineup full-time.

In 2001 the team moved one step closer by beating the Phoenix Suns in the first round, before getting destroyed by the Shaq-Kobe Lakers in the second round. After the season, in July of 2001, the team made the semi-controversial decision to trade Jason Williams to the Grizzlies for Mike Bibby. Many fans in Sacramento were heartbroken to see "White Chocolate" leave town. The Grizzlies wanted Williams to sell tickets. The Kings wanted Bibby to put them over the top.

The night of the trade was one of the great nights of all time for local sports radio. I was working security and listening to sports-talk radio literally all night long. I heard a woman crying and feeling betrayed because the Maloofs had said they didn't plan to trade Williams and then did. Many other fans had similar reactions. Casual basketball fans really really loved him because he was so exciting to watch. Some, however (like me), were very excited because we knew that Bibby was a much better player.

Bibby would go on to be everything the team had hoped for and then some.

That summer, the Kings also re-signed Webber to a maximum contract after much stress. Before Webber took the offer, he played the field and met with several other teams. He wanted to leave this small town and this was his chance. The season before, he had watched the first truly amazing free-agent class (which included Tim Duncan, Grant Hill, Tracy McGrady and others, all in the primes of their careers) be courted endlessly and get the red-carpet treatment by several cities. This time around, teams had learned their lessons and were not doing the same things. Webber was shocked that no other team gave him an easy option to leave so he eventually came back to the Kings. *Webber reluctantly took the Kings' 80-plus million dollars to stay.*

The move was great for the team at the time, as it ensured that the team would have a window of championship contention. There was a famous billboard locally in which the Maloofs offered to mow Webber's lawn if he stayed. The team had done everything possible to get their star to stay. *Back when the Maloofs seemed to know what they were doing.*

Back on the court, the team was now fully loaded at every position. They were now elite. Night after night they ran teams right out of the building. They finished with a league-best record of 61–21 in 2001-02. They had taken the next step and in the playoffs did so as well, making it past the second round and into the Western Conference finals. There, they would again face, and lose to, the Lakers.

APPENDIX 6
THE FIX IS IN

The 2002 Kings-Lakers playoffs series went on to become one of the most famous series of all time. In Game 3, Mike Bibby had the guts to take and make one of the biggest shots in team history, coming around a screen and nailing a mid-range jumper in heroic fashion. Gavin Maloof exploded out of his seat and the building nearly exploded. The team went up 2-1 and was poised to take Game 4 in the closing seconds until they faced the bad end of a historic play. The Kings led by two with seven seconds to play. Kobe attacked the rim and was stopped. Shaq got the ball at close range and missed, before Divac batted the ball out to the perimeter with about two seconds to go. Somehow, some way, the ball went straight to 'big-shot' Robert Horry, who gave the Kings the worst stomach punch of their lives by draining the open three. I remember this moment like it was this morning. The feeling is indescribable. It was like the ultimate instant shock experience ever. In literally the blink of an eye, the Kings went from almost certainly going to the NBA Finals, to being back in the thick of one of the most contested series in history.

Instead of taking a 3-1 lead, the Kings lost 100-99 and went to 2-2 in the series. If Horry missed that shot the Kings would have certainly won the series and then the NBA title. This was one of the biggest shots of all time... and the Kings came up on the bad end of it.

The Kings won game five to go up 3-2 in the series and set the stage for the historic game six, which came to be known by most as one of the most clearly fixed games ever. The game featured many, many questionable calls. One of the most egregious came on a play late in the fourth quarter. After a Kings' score, the Lakers tried to inbound the ball to Kobe Bryant, who was being defended fiercely by Mike Bibby. (*The first and last time in his life Bibby played any defense.*) To escape Bibby, Bryant elbowed Bibby in the face, sending him to the floor. Bryant dribbled down the court and the Lakers got a score as Bibby slowly came to his senses and got up with a bloody face. The foul was obvious to everyone in real time, but looked even worse on television as replays repeatedly showed Bibby get hit and go down. No foul was called, but even Laker fans knew what happened. In a series between the two best teams in the NBA in which both teams complained about the officiating every game, in game six it was clear: the playing field was not even.

Presidential candidate Ralph Nader issued a public statement that ran in the local paper and elsewhere:

"At a time when the public's confidence is shaken by headlines reporting the breach of trust by corporate executives, it is important... for there to be maintained a sense of impartiality and professionalism in commercial sports performances... That sense was severely shaken in the now notorious officiating during Game 6 of the Western Conference Finals between the Los Angeles Lakers and the Sacramento Kings... When (Washington post writer Michael) Wilbon writes that 'The Kings and Lakers didn't decide this series ...three referees did...' When many thousands of fans, not just those in Sacramento, felt that merit lost to bad refereeing, you need to take notice beyond the usual and widespread grumbling by fans and columnists about referees ignoring the rule book and giving advantages to home teams and superstars." [6]

Wilbon's full comments that Nader alluded to were, "I still consider [Game 6] the single worst-officiated game in the 28 years I've been covering professional basketball. It was egregiously, embarrassingly bad ... Stern and the NBA had better deal with it quickly, lest they appear completely unaware of a condition that will threaten the credibility of the league." [7]

Then-ESPN NBA guru David Aldridge was quoted, "there is nothing I can say that will explain 27 free throws for the Lakers in the fourth quarter, an amount staggering in its volume and impact on the game. It gave me pause. How can you explain it? How can you explain a game where Scott Pollard fouls out when he's two feet from Shaquille O'Neal, or that Doug Christie is called for a ridiculous touch foul just as Chris Webber spikes Bryant's drive to the hoop, or that Mike Bibby is called for a foul deep in the fourth quarter after Bryant pops him in the nose with an elbow?" [8]

To top it all off, in 2008 disgraced former NBA referee Tim Donaghy said in court papers that Game 6 was fixed by the NBA. Donaghy wrote, "Sacramento had the best team in the league... but the referees/league didn't allow the better team to win." Then, in his book *Personal Foul*, Donaghy wrote that, "As soon as the referees for the game were chosen for game 6, the rest of us [other NBA refs] knew immediately there would be a

Game 7." Asked to elaborate, Donaghy wrote me that "Bavetta would always say he was the NBA's 'go to guy' and he would always help make the series go another game … he said [this] to me before the game in L.A."

True enough, Donaghy is a referee who fixed games himself, which obviously discredits him and makes his words suspect, but combined with all the other evidence, it adds up. For the NBA's part, Lawrence Pedowitz, who led a review of the league's officiating following the outbreak of the scandal, concluded that while Game 6 was poorly officiated, no concrete evidence existed of that game being fixed.

Also, Samaki Walker's three-pointer just before halftime of game four (that replays clearly showed came after the buzzer) led to the NBA instituting instant replay the following season.

While I just spent half a page explaining that the Kings were robbed (which they were!), I am also the first to admit that the Kings shouldn't have won anyway and perhaps even deserved to lose. They were the better team that year but they flat-out choked in Game 6 and 7. Whatever the referees did, they didn't make the Kings choke the game away at the free throw line and from the field. They didn't make the Kings miss 14 of 30 free throws in Game 7. They did that all on their own. They missed shots that they should have made easily. I can still remember, in particular, missed shots by Doug Christie and Peja Stojakovic that burn the deepest corners of my mind. Christie had a look at an open three-pointer from straight-on that missed the rim entirely and clanged the backboard so hard I thought it might shatter. Peja air-balled a wide-open three-pointer from the corner that he would normally make. Corrupt officials or not, the Kings had a chance and they didn't get it done. That is on them.

The Kings lost Games 6 and 7, as well as their best chance at a title. Despite the devastating loss, the Kings were still contenders moving forward and hoped to come back the next season and set things right. *Webber's knees (and guts) would not let that happen.*

In the 02-03 season the team went 59-23 and won their division. They were a well-oiled machine primed for a title run. After cruising through the first round of the playoffs, in the second round disaster struck. Chris Webber went down with a knee injury. At first, Webber declared, "I'll be back for game four next series." His statement was premature. Without Webber, the Kings went on to lose in seven games and end their season.

Webber's injury signaled the end of everything the Kings had accomplished.

The following year, Webber missed most of the season recovering from the injury. Without him, however, the team thrived during the regular season and Stojakovic went to the next level, finishing second only to Tracy McGrady for the scoring title. Still, coach Adelman forced Webber back into the lineup before he was ready, believing that the team could not win a championship without him. Webber returned, played horribly, destroyed the Kings free-flowing offense and chemistry that had developed in his absence, and led to a second-round playoff loss to the Minnesota Timberwolves. *Fittingly, Webber missed the last shot in game six of that series as well.*

In the 2004-05 season the Kings run officially ended. An aging Vlade Divac signed with the Lakers. Doug Christie was traded to the Orlando Magic. Then, Webber was traded to the Philadelphia 76ers for spare parts, officially signaling the end of the line.

Just as the team was built and had progressed in an optimum fashion into a contender, the team's demise was equally painful and slow. From there, the team made the playoffs one more time before spending the next few years spiraling down the toilet with one bad move after another, leading to the Kings current status as one of the three worst teams in the NBA. (Although that is about to change.)

At a fan event in 2010 I got to meet then-coach Paul Westphal. It is one of my only positive Kings memories from a horrible era in the team's history. (The Westphal regime went down in flames, like almost everything else the Maloofs touched around this time).

APPENDIX 7
THE DOLLARS MAKE SENSE

For those who don't care about basketball, let this section be a reason to care about the issue. This section is all about the money.

One of the key aspects of this whole thing is economics. Arenas impact cities, regions and even states more than most people realize. Some of the indicators are obvious. People who live in a city where a new arena is built can see it with their own eyes. And soon too shall Sacramento. They can see the bars, sports clubs, restaurants, hotels and other companies that come along with an arena. But some of the indicators are not so obvious. This is why it can be very hard to see the impact an arena makes on every single person. There are strong voices in favor of publicly-financed arenas and there are just as many who believe the local spending would go to other entertainment options if there was no team (something economists call, "substitution spending"). *This is a tough argument to make in Sacramento, because there are almost no other entertainment options to consider.*

For years people around here have asked me how the arena impacts them and why they should care. My answer has always been that arenas affect the economy and the economy affects every single person in the region (and further). Just as any large construction of any kind or any business can completely shape a local economy, sports arenas are a business that helps circulate hundreds of million dollars into the local economy thereby affecting every single person. If you ask me specifically, 'does this affect me?' my answer is always 'yes'.

How bad are things in Sacramento? As of summer 2013, the unemployment rate is 9.8 percent, down from 13 percent in 2010. This is substantial improvement but still far worse than the national average of 7.4 percent. One of the biggest problems has been a shrinking government workforce due to steady budget cuts. The government sector, even after shrinking through spending cuts and layoffs in recent years, still accounts for nearly 28 percent of the local labor market. Everyone in town knows about "furlough Fridays" and all the other budget drama that makes a huge impact on the city. Sacramento's average gas price is $3.89 per gallon, compared with the national average of $3.62. These are just a couple of indicators of how the city economy is doing. After a booming economy during the first half of the last decade, Sacramento's economic output has fallen for six consecutive years.

In 2009 Sacramento gained unfortunate attention for what came to be called "Tent City." Though the area that housed these tents has been fenced off and the families moved, the problem only got worse. Many formerly middle class families have been forced out of their homes and the city has been struggling with this problem ever since. At its peak, Tent City was home to over 200 residents. Even Oprah Winfrey, the Today Show and CNN did episodes about it. Many people have tried to present ideas about what to do with the homeless, how to help them, and how to keep something like Tent City from happening again. Still, there are places around town where people in tents gather. Some find room on the river, under overpasses, run-down parks and anywhere else they can find space where they will not be hassled. While Tent City is gone, the homelessness problem rages on.

A new arena is not going to solve all these problems, but it will help a lot.

In the case of any NBA arena, there are financial, capital, and intellectual ramifications rooted in the standard of living for the area. Having a professional sports team in any town can provide a stronger economy due to the job creation, out-of-town visitors spending money, and reputation of an area. Examples of jobs that come in higher demand include: janitors, valets, ticket brokers, ushers ticket-takers, food service workers, and security personnel. These employees typically earn $9 an hour on average. There are also at least three years of construction jobs, the possibility of more companies choosing to have offices in the city, and the 'multiplier effect' which suggests that increased local income causes more spending and job creation. It should also be considered that there are people that make their living from basketball games, both partially and completely. Restaurants, food-service companies, souvenir shops, and even street performers benefit from being in the center of an area of people with expendable income.

According to some studies being done in Sacramento, "the entertainment and sports complex will generate over $157 million in revenue for the entire region on an annual basis, including $100 million in downtown Sacramento, $116 million in the City of Sacramento, $131 million in the County of Sacramento and $157 million in the greater Sacramento region. The facility's operating costs will be covered by the direct revenue generated within the arena, over a thirty year period the Sacramento region will receive over $7 billion in economic activity. An Entertainment and Sports Complex will attract 3.1 million new visitors to Downtown Sacramento on an annual basis. Hotels located within walking distance of the facility in Downtown Sacramento will see an increase of over 300,000 guests who choose to spend at least one night in a downtown hotel. Fiscal benefits for government agencies created by 3.1 million new visitors will include approximately $6.7 million annually generated by $5.8 million in sales taxes and over $900,000 in transient occupancy taxes. Additional revenue would be expected to be generated by increases in other sources of government revenue such as property taxes." [9]

On the other side, there are those who preach against the value of sports franchises. In 2000 a study by the Cato Institute failed to identify a single case of a professional sports team increasing its host cities' economy. Detractors also suggest that the money residents spend on sports teams is money that they would be spending on other things if there were no team. There is also the idea that most players do not reside in the cities they play in, meaning that in most cases, the millions they make in salary are spent in other cities. Some also point out that most stadium and arena employees work part-time and make low wages. *Even if all of this is true, common sense still says that the arenas and teams help the city.*

While few conclusions can be reached, the general effect of the most recent arenas built for NBA teams serve as loose examples of the potential impact of an arena.

Example 1: Oklahoma City

Oklahoma City represents the closest and best example to compare to Sacramento, as it is similar in size and notoriety. Most importantly, it is the only other city besides Sacramento and Salt Lake City in which the NBA is the only major sports franchise in its city or surrounding areas.

Chesapeake Energy Arena (as it is now called) in Oklahoma City opened on June 8, 2002, three years after construction began. The 581,000-square-foot building seats up to 19,675 on three seating levels with a fourth added during concerts. It features 3,380 club seats, seven party suites and 49 private suites. It is located immediately across the street from the Cox Convention Center, which is a 15,000 seat arena in its own right. The arena was paid for by a local tax that generated over $89 million to build the structure. In March of 2008, Oklahoma City taxpayers (residents) approved a temporary one-cent sales tax to go toward improvements to the Oklahoma City Arena (now called Chesapeake Energy Arena), along with an off-site practice facility for the Thunder. (*How the city approved the tax is a story for another author. I only know that Sacramento never approved and never would have approved such a tax*).

The sales tax, which began in January of 2009, lasted for 15 months. Improvements to the Oklahoma City Arena included a new grand entrance, multistory atrium, additional restaurants and clubs at every level, bunker suites, loge and sky boxes, roof top gardens, locker rooms, a warm-up basketball court, team offices, a 12,000-square-foot family activity center, and other

NBA specific improvements. Support of the temporary sales tax to upgrade the Oklahoma City Arena and construct a new NBA practice facility largely contributed to the Thunder making Oklahoma City their home. Capital funding for arena improvements and the new practice facility amounted to approximately $48,295,444 in the 2011-2012 fiscal year, and 93.1 million dollars. Through a simple tax. The new and improved Chesapeake Energy Arena was 100 percent publicly financed using a one percent sales tax (Munsey & Suppes).

In 2010, OKC officials did a basic study and based their Thunder impact estimates on data collected during the New Orleans Hornets' temporary stay in Oklahoma. This is a highly subjective way to look at it, however using this methodology they say that OKC is looking at more than $53 million in economic impact per year.

Locals say that the people of a suburb of OKC called Altus and many towns just like it make the 130 or-more-mile drive from southwest Oklahoma for every Thunder home game at Chesapeake Energy Arena. They estimate that dozens of families do something similar. This serves as a small example of how far-reaching the impact of an arena and a sports franchise can have. The fact that people will travel two hours each way 41 times a year to spend their money there says a lot. Up until 2012, city officials estimated the team's economic impact at $1.2 million per game. This year, that figure went up to a whopping $1.5 million. Multiply that number by the minimum 41 home games per year and then consider how much of that money is coming from outside the actual city and you can start to get a picture of how much money an NBA team brings into a city. Many suggest the figures are actually too low, as it does not include employment at the arena or restaurants and hotels that can be attributed to the games. The formula used by the city (provided by the Destination Marketing Association International) further estimates that for each in-town guest (those who travel within metro area) will spend $65, compared to those outside the metro area, who are expected to spend $216. In a growing city like OKC (or say, Sacramento...) this is the kind of economic impact that can completely change a city.

To be fair, some suggest that much of the spending is not new money, it is money being shifted from other entertainment spending.

There is further evidence suggesting the impact of an arena and NBA team here. After the SuperSonics left Seattle the economy there decreased by roughly $12,004,000. On the other side, the Thunder's new home in Oklahoma City saw its economy grow immensely. Oklahoma City's economy generated an additional $525,665,535 in the first year after the Thunder arrived. This increase represents a 7 percent jump from pre-NBA levels. (*To be fair, many measures indicated that the OKC economy was already on the rise when the Thunder got there, but the impact is obvious.*) The team also generates millions of dollars in sales of Thunder merchandise: jerseys, apparel, and other memorabilia – over $100,000,000.

That number is chump change compared to what Sacramento fans will spend in the next four years.

However you look at it, it would be very difficult to say that
Oklahoma City is not better off having the Thunder and their
arena.

Example 2: Indiana

*T*he next best example is Conseco Fieldhouse in Indianapolis, where the NBA's Pacers play. In 2010, *Hunden Strategic Partners* was commissioned to fully explore the economic impact of the Pacers on the city. Their study concluded that if the Pacers were to leave Indiana, the following economic changes could be expected, even after accounting for the $15-16 million it costs to operate the building every year: $55 million annual net loss of economic activity in Indianapolis, $17.8 million annual net loss to Indianapolis Government Bodies (fiscal impact), 909 Permanent Full-Time Equivalent Jobs lost and up to 25 million per year in lost television revenue and arena naming rights. This is just one study and one city, but one that is quite similar to Sacramento in many ways, including population density, market size and location. Indiana is one example of a place that got its arena deal done right and is a model of sorts for new buildings going up around the NBA. It is also a clear example of what a city might stand to lose if its team left them.

Example 3: Charlotte

Time Warner Cable Arena (originally Charlotte Bobcats Arena) is an entertainment and sports venue, built and located in the center of the city of Charlotte, North Carolina. The building is home to the NBA's Charlotte Bobcats. It made its opening in October 2005, with a concert by The Rolling Stones. It hosted its first Bobcats game on November 5, 2005.

The arena seats 19,077 for NBA games, but can be expanded to seat up to 20,200 for college basketball games (*and NBA playoff games if the team ever makes the playoffs*).

The arena was constructed with the Bobcats in mind, but it also hosts many types of sports and entertainment events. In addition to the Bobcats, the arena is also currently home to the Charlotte Checkers of the ECHL and host many rodeo and NASCAR promotional events.

The arena was originally intended to host the Charlotte Hornets, the city's original NBA team. In 2001, a non-binding public referendum for an arts package, which included money to build the new uptown arena, was placed on the ballot for voters. Voters rejected the city bond referendum that would have spent $205 million on a new arena for the Charlotte Hornets, plus millions more for arts projects. The NBA team said it was losing money on the Charlotte Coliseum, which opened in 1988 on Tyvola Road.

In 2002, the Hornets announced they would move to New Orleans. That November, the Charlotte City Council voted to put $265 million toward a new arena uptown to bring in a new NBA franchise.

Opponents at the time said the city was spending too much for a professional sports league and objected to the council's decision to go forward with an arena when the city's residents had voted against it. Other arena opponents still feel the investment was an error. They suggest that the coliseum on Tyvola Road would still have been a draw for most of the events that Time Warner Cable Arena now hosts. They also criticize the decision to let the Bobcats benefit from profits made from other events there.

Those who support the arena point to how the arena contributes to uptown and the economic impact of events like the Democratic National Convention and all the big-draw concerts that the arena now hosts as indications that the city's investment has paid off. Other local leaders say there is $3.9 billion of development going on in uptown, about half of which is attributable to the arena. That includes the creation of the 210 Trade Apartments, along with the Courtside Apartments and the Ritz Carlton Hotel.

Clearly, there is evidence to support both sides in the case of Charlotte. Still, it is an example of how arenas can be built and serves as some indication of the impact of an arena on a city.

Example 4: Orlando

One last example of arena building comes in a different situation. One of the most recently built arenas in the NBA is The Amway Center in Orlando, Florida, home of the Orlando Magic and the Orlando Predators of the AFL. This building was opened on September 29th, 2010. It is located in the heart of downtown Florida, maximizing the economic advantages it provides. It came to be as part of something called, "Downtown Orlando Master Plan 3." The plan involved construction of the Amway Center for around $500 million, upgrades and maintenance to the Citrus Bowl for $175 million, and a performing arts center for $375 million. The whole thing came to be called the "Triple crown of downtown."

As in the other cities in need of new buildings, it took more than ten years of maneuvering to make this one happen. The financing came from a combination of team investment, city bonds and naming rights. Incredibly, the team was able to secure a 10 year, $40 million contract for those naming rights. The team advanced $50 million and paid for the majority of the cost of the building, while the city provided the land and infrastructure. The time from approval of the deal to the opening of the building was between 2 1/2-3 years (depending when you start counting from). The building is state of the art in basically every way and is a model for how the NBA wants cities and teams to build their arenas.

The impact of the arena is mixed on this one as well. Some point to a series of failed attempts at building restaurants around

Amway Center (while others blame lawmakers for that). On the other hand, the arena did pretty well, bringing in $998,913 in operating net income in its first year of existence. The arena also hosted the 2012 NBA All-Star game and gained over $95 million in economic benefit from that alone (orlandosentinal. com).

This is an example of how stadiums and arenas can do great things for communities when they bring in visitors from out of town. This is especially valuable in a city like Orlando that boasts many other tourist attractions as well. Still, the effects of an arena are tempered if the community is paying huge sums each year to finance the facility.

I cannot say with certainty that the new arena in Sacramento will be a boon to the economy, since no one has been able to unequivocally prove and measure the true economic impact of an arena. That said, in the cases of the most recent arenas, especially those in cities similar to Sacramento, the effects can clearly be seen. At a very minimum, cities seem to come out at least a bit ahead financially when they build arenas. Their value does not just come in money. There is prestige, civic pride, the possibility of expanded tourism and a hundred other things that simply cannot be measured.

There is a small chance that this will all go bad due to poor management or corruption in the city building process. There is also a very very good chance that this will all turn out great and change the city for the better forever. On a risk-reward scale, this whole thing is almost preposterous that we even have to debate whether or not this is a good idea. It's a no-brainer.

APPENDIX 8
DAVID STERN

*D*avid Stern will go down as, arguably, the greatest commissioner in sports history. When he took over the league, NBA Finals games were shown on tape delay and no games were available outside the U.S. As he retires in 2014 he leaves the league as a multi-billion dollar industry, set up fantastically for the next decade (*largely due to helping the owners behead the players' union and embarrassing them in the negotiations of 2011*).

APPENDIX 9
THE MEMORIES

In 1993 my dad and I went to a Kings game on a fateful Tuesday night. I can't remember the opponent anymore. A lot of the night is a blur. My dad and I were in our seats as the first quarter was being played. Over the loudspeakers we heard the announcement that one lucky fan's seat would be chosen at random to shoot a shot from half-court to win a new car. I thought nothing of it. The arena had a capacity of 17,137 with a sold-out game. With our two tickets, my dad and I had a 1/8568.5 chance of being selected. I wasn't holding my breath. Still, earlier that day, I had joked with my neighbor (Kelly Scott) about how cool it would be if that happened as we shot hoops at his house. As the voice came through over the loudspeakers, the seat numbers were called out and other people in our row began to get excited. Sure enough, my seat was selected. My dad looked at me in bewilderment, shocked at what we had just stumbled into and wondering if I was up for it. On one hand, I was a high school kid and an immature one at that. On the other hand, I had spent months practicing the half court shot during lunch at school.

I had shot and made that shot hundreds of times. I was very nervous, but absolutely up for it. The attendant came to our row and found us and confirmed it was me. My dad called home to have my step-mom record the game (on VHS!) in case they showed it. Sometime early in the second quarter the attendant came back and took my dad and I underneath the building and around to the end of the court in the tunnel. I was to shoot the shot during halftime festivities. The time came and an usher walked me out to half court. As we passed, Kings center Duane Causwell yelled to me, "aim for the backboard." I laughed and thought it was awesome that a Kings player spoke to me. *I also thought it was silly because I was not going to hit the backboard, I was going to make this shot!* I got to the line, rotated the ball from the front all the way around into an overhand passing motion (just as I had done so many times at school). At that moment I thought it was meant to be. My shot flew through the air and the crowd gasped as my shot appeared to be on line. On that old VHS tape they don't show it, but you can hear the roar in the background as Napear and Reynolds did their half-time show. My shot came up just short and to the left, glancing the net as it sailed to the ground. In life there are so many "what-ifs." In mine, this was a great one. Five inches higher and to the right with my shot and I would have had a car. *Instead, I got a Kings hat.* The next day at school one person had seen it, Mr. Clark, my GSR teacher. I came into second period that day and he said he had seen me and told some other bewildered classmates. That was pretty much the end of it and my life moved on.

ACKNOWLEDGMENTS

The idea for this book was born in my mind nearly 25 years ago. At various times in the last three years I thought the title of this book might be, "How Sacramento lost the Kings." That didn't happen. I got to write the happy story of how my city did something special. Many people helped me either personally or symbolically and I want to acknowledge them.

Special thanks to:

*Z*ackary Coldiron for giving me my purpose. Gerrit Thompson and Victor Alfieri for helping me shape my words into the best story I could tell. Greg 'DJgrandtheft' Taylor for inspiring the chapter about fans' responsibility. Zeb Wheeler for research help and being awesome. Patrick Lucas for photos. Brett Bulbrandson for ideas. Cindy Thomas for inspiration. Jon Tobin and Derek Rauh for being badass. Everyone living with Tourette's syndrome (as I do). Everyone who ever listened to Sports 1140 radio or called in to talk to the likes of Napear, Kozimor, Ross, Redd, the Rise Guys, Rob Arnie and Dawn, Carmichael Dave and others over the years. And all the fans and citizens in Sacramento that understood why this matters. We all did it together and we all have a chance to do great things in the next few years. I hope this book can be one of many ways we continue to show the world what kind of city and what kind of people we are. I hope I can find more ways to help.

To the dozens of people to whom I tried to explain the situation and who did not understand. They are one of the biggest reasons I wrote this book. Tom Wold who, in particular, frustrated me so badly with his misunderstanding that I decided I absolutely had to write this book.

To Mayor Kevin Johnson... for everything. Grant Napear for always telling us how it is, Carmichael Dave for telling us how it could be, and Vivek Ranadive for showing us that it will be. (*Much love to ya, Mr. Ranadive*) Mitch Richmond, Scott

Pollard, Jon Barry, Bobby Jackson, Lionell Simmons, Lawrence Funderburke, Vlade Divac and other Kings who represented the essence of what the team and the city of Sacramento are all about in the best possible ways. Tough, determined, hardworking, team-first, reliable and enthusiastic. You have helped shape the identity of the city and the team, leading to what we are today. *(And to Pervis Ellison, who is literally getting dunked on at this very moment.)*

To Chris Webber, for being the complete opposite of the group above and for being the anti-hero the city needed. *(And will always need)*

To the memory of William Coldiron, who would have loved this book most of all.

And to Price World Publishing for giving me the means to tell my story.

REFERENCES

1 http://www.reviewjournal.com/sports/basketball/after-kings-sale-gavin-maloof-says-hes-glad-team-staying-sacramento
2 http://newsok.com/sonics-owners-e-mails/article/3783093
3 http://cowbellkingdom.com/2013/04/23/the-nba-shouldnt-buy-the-maloofs-version-of-the-sacramento-kings-narrative/
4 http://archive2.capradio.org/articles/2013/05/15/transcript-mayor-kevin-johnson,-vivek-ranadive-and-mark-friedman-press-conference/
5 http://www.usatoday.com/story/sports/nba/2013/05/15/seattle-still-without-nba-after-relocation-denied/2164701/
6 http://www.leagueoffans.org/sternletter.html
7 http://www.thedailybeast.com/articles/2012/06/06/the-nba-s-greatest-ugliest-series.html
8 http://en.wikipedia.org/wiki/National_Basketball_Association_criticisms_and_controversies
9 http://downtownarena.org/category/facts-about-the-arena/